Global Economy
under Geopolitical Change

Global Economy under Geopolitical Change

First printing edition September 26th, 2024

Author Myoung Soo KIM
Translated by Jackie Jiyeon Lee
Publisher Gil Su Jang
Distributed in South Korea by Knowledge and Sensibility*
Publication Registration 2012-000081

Address 1212, 50-3 Dearung 6. Gasan-dong, Geumcheon-gu, Seoul
Phone 070-4651-3730 to 4
Fax 070-4325-7006
Email ksbookup@naver.com
Website www.knsbookup.com

ISBN 979-11-392-2182-4(03320)
price 18,000won

Please approach seller for the exchange of books with printing errors.
The use of all or part of this book and its contents will require prior permission from the copyright holder and the publisher.

Global Economy
under Geopolitical Change

Myoung Soo KIM

NICE
INVESTORS SERVICE

CONTENTS

PREFACE —————————————————————— 6

PART 1. Change of Global Economy

Global Economic Implications of the Russia-Ukraine War — 12

A New Solution for a New Cold War ————————— 40

Korean Economy Searching for Its Way Forward ————— 58

Nationalization of China's Real Estate
Sector and Europe's Role ———————————————— 83

Implications of the Financial Blockade
against China and the Onset of Monetary Easing ———— 99

PART 2. Change of International Politics

US-China Competition for Greater Power Becomes Systemic —— 114

Shifting U.S. Middle East Policy —— 136

Netanyahu Ignites the Powder Keg Waiting to Blow —— 147

The Potential Impact of Trump's Return —— 154

PART 3. Changes in Industries

A New Sweeping Wave of Antitrust Aimed at Big Tech —— 178

Europe's Descent into Deindustrialization —— 206

High Oil Prices and Weak Yen Cast Shadow —— 224

Watching out for the Resurgence of Japan's Electronics Industry (Part I) —— 244

Watching out for the Resurgence of Japan's Electronics Industry (Part II) —— 267

COMPUTEX TAIPEI 2024 From a Geopolitical Perspective —— 293

PREFACE

Korea grew into the world's fifth-largest industrialized country and seventh-largest trading nation, riding on free trade under the GATT system led by the United States during the Cold War. In order to understand the past and the future of Korean economy, therefore it is essential to look into the international trade environment.

Stimulated by the export-led growth of South Korea and neighboring East Asian countries, Chinese economy grew fast and its economic output has reached up to 70% of the U.S. economy. In 2018, the U.S. government launched a trade war against China in competition for global hegemony, and since then the global trade environment has been changing rapidly. For 30 years until the 1990s, Korea thrived on direct exports to the U.S. market, which was then followed by another 3 decades of growth by indirect exports via China. Both eras were relatively peaceful, but now Korean companies are faced with a trade environment that they have never seen in the past 60 years.

Since the outbreak of the Ukraine War in February 2022, international politics and world economy has been going through precipitous changes. The Fed repeatedly raised interest rates to combat inflation and global investors moved money into the U.S. market. Central banks around the world rushed to raise interest rates as well to defend the exchange rate, whereupon the international financial market agitated.

However, a fundamental change beyond the financial market chaos lies in the fact that the Russia-Ukraine War has divided the world economy into two blocs: the West vs. China and Russia. The West with technology and capital is breaking apart with China and Russia that have strong manufacturing and rich resources, and each bloc is put to the test whether it could survive on its own.

For 75 years after the World War II, the global economy worked on David Ricardo's comparative advantage theory, mobilizing all the available resources, labor, technology, and capital to supply consumers with quality products at affordable prices. Now, the West, led by the United States, has made it clear that it will no longer provide technology and capital to the China and Russia bloc, and that the United States, Europe, and Japan will take over advanced manufacturing capabilities, and that Russian resources will be traded at much lower price than the international rates.

Now that the global economy is divided into 'buyers' and 'sellers' as a result of the 75 years of endeavor to maximize efficiency, what will the final outcome be, and on which side should Korea stand? The bargaining power of buyers and sellers in the commodity market may vary depending on time and conditions, but the winner is always the 'buyer' in the end. Buyers create international standards and norms, and sellers are to conform to those norms. Korea is a seller, but has no choice but to join the ranks of buyers.

As the head of a credit rating agency, I have been trying to provide financial market participants with insights into the intricate changes in the international economic environment since 2020. The four years of deliberations are compiled into a book. I hope this book will provide helpful guidance to readers who are at loss in the vast landscape of international politics, economy, and industry.

September 1, 2024
Myoung Soo KIM

PART 1
Change of Global Economy

Global Economy under Geopolitical Change

Global Economic Implications of the Russia-Ukraine War[1]

1. Changes that the Russia-Ukraine War Has Brought

1) The Long-standing Dream of Ukraine

As much as Taiwan and the Korean Peninsula can be described as a powder keg in East Asia, the most conflict-prone regions in Europe have been the Ukraine and three Baltic countries – Lithuania, Latvia, and Estonia. In 1989, Gorbachev of the Soviet Union agreed to German reunification on the condition that NATO would not expand eastward to the Warsaw Pact countries. Poland, the Czech Republic and Hungary had a painful history of being invaded by Soviet troops and they wanted to join the prospering EU. So the agreement was ignored. (They formally joined NATO in 1999 for its first round of expansion).

The problem arose in 2004, when the second round of

---

[1] This column was published on March 28, 2022.

NATO expansion took place. The three Baltic countries that were the republics of the former Soviet Union and whose national survival had been in question, joined NATO. At that time, Russia was disintegrating with Kaliningrad isolated. The country torn apart was unable to do anything even when NATO deployed a small group of forces serving as tripwires in the three Baltic states.

Russian President Putin, who had succeeded in rehabilitating the country with stabilization of the oil industry, made the landmark speech at the Munich Security Conference in 2007 right before stepping down to the prime minister due to the constitutional limit of consecutive presidential terms. In the speech he denounced the United States and NATO member states saying NATO's advance into Eastern Europe would no longer be tolerated. He meant Ukraine. Five years later in 2012, Putin returned to the presidency and he made it clear that the Ukraine-NATO issue was non-negotiable.

Ukraine, a new independent country born in 1991, was in the process of finding a national identity. The territory was split into east and west by the Dnieper River, Ukrainian and Russian languages were mixed, and the nation was divided into pro-Russian and pro-Western. Such conflicts over the political stance has led to the Euromaidan Revolution in the winter of 2013. The protest were the choice of the Ukrainian people who were pro-Western. After that, the pro-Russian government was ousted and Ukraine's joining NATO membership was written in its constitution. Russia took action in 2014 and occupied Crimea.

Despite Ukraine's constant courting it was not allowed to join NATO. Until June 2021, NATO member states repeatedly said that Ukraine had to meet the conditions for membership, but on November 10 last year, the United States made a far more advanced promise, signing a strategic partnership with Ukraine to support Ukraine's accession to NATO. Putin took this as the crossing of the red line and began preparing for war in December. And on February 24 of this year, the war broke out.

2) Difference between Trump and Biden Administrations

President Donald Trump, whose bid for the second term failed, pursued "America first" policy through energy independence and the revival of manufacturing during his presidency, and his foreign policy was summarized as "anti-China". To that end Trump needed to neutralize Russia, so he tried to form a friendly relation with America's traditional enemy Russia.

Trump's policies have spawned many international conflicts. He denounced the protective trade polices of Germany, Japan, and South Korea that belong to world's largest exporting countries and revised free trade agreements, and explicitly demanded them to pay more for US troops stationed in the countries. He clashed with German and French leaders at the summit meeting, demanding the NATO partners raise their defense expenditure to match with their economic size. Furthermore, he pressed EU countries to join his anti-China campaign, emphatically saying China poses a great threat to the world order.

Such demands provoked backlash from EU countries, especially Germany. German Chancellor Angela Merkel, who formed a coalition with the Social Democrats who was negative on defense spending, expressed her displeasure at the demand and also Germany was not in a position to sanction China, the biggest export market for German companies. In fact, Trump's demands were rather far-fetched for European countries. China is geographically far-off and it is only a threat of distant future that China determines the world order. China, taking note of these sentiments, has been implementing a European-friendly foreign policy.

Germany protested when Trump demanded to call off the Nord Stream II Baltic Sea gas pipe line project which was nearing completion. This pipeline was an alternative for Germany that has been pushing hard for nuclear phase-out and de-carbonization since 2011 and it also symbolized Germany's engagement policy with Russia. Germany thought that expanding exchanges with Russia would spur economic growth of Russia and help it adapt to free trade, and then liberal democracy would gradually set foot in Russia to make it a peace-loving country. The engagement policy wasn't a new idea. It was already the cornerstone of Britain's Russia policy.

U.S. President Joe Biden reaffirmed U.S. fealty to the transatlantic alliance saying "America is back," at the Munich Security Conference in February 2021, a month after he took office. It has been unclear what this really means. However, with the Russia-Ukraine War which is even dubbed as "Europe's 9/11," it is becoming clearer.

3) The U.S. and Europe Becoming One

When the war in Ukraine broke out on February 24, 2022, the United States and Europe united to impose economic sanctions on Russia although they had drawn a line that they would not send troops. The first action they took was financial sanctions. Russia's seven largest banks were banned from SWIFT - the main dollar payment network - except for Gazprom bank, and Russian central bank was shut off from access to most of its foreign reserves deposited in the US and Western central banks. The second restrictive measure against Russia was cutting their business ties. BP and Shell in the UK and Exxon Mobil in the US have announced to sell off their stakes and pull their business from Russia. Consumer goods giants such as Apple, Coca-Cola and McDonald's have suspended business operations in Russia. The third step is the US embargo on Russian oil, and Europe, as well, is considering a ban on Russian oil and gas imports.

Germany was unusually quick to join the sanctions against Russia, which is quite surprising considering its past political record. German Chancellor Olaf Scholz has announced a halt to the Nord Stream II gas pipeline project in which 11 billion dollars has already been invested, and decided to fast track the construction of two LNG terminals, which had been lukewarm until now. Economic Minister Robert Habeck secured the accord during his visit to Qatar on long-term LNG supplies from Qatar to Germany.

For the first time Germany reversed its historic policy of never getting involved in any military conflict since the World War II, providing non-lethal equipment to Ukraine. And it declared an increase of defense spending from 1.5% to 2% of its GDP and modernization of the armed forces by issuing 100 billion euros of government bonds. The decision was made just two days after the war by the coalition government of Social Democrats who are reluctant to increase defense spending; the Green Party that is against any investment in fossil fuels; and the LDP which is not in favor of the issuance of government bonds.

The Russian ruble plummeted, the stock market crashed, and international settlements were put to a halt. Russia's second moratorium was just around the corner. Expecting backlash from the US and Europe, Putin has long strengthened a friendship with Chinese President Xi Jinping. The troops sent to Ukraine were based in Vladivostok. The risky strategy of withdrawing troops from eastern Siberia and Primorsky Krai, which China has been eyeing, suggests a trust between the leaders of China and Russia. U.S. President Biden has issued a stern warning against Chinese President Xi Jinping that if China helps Russia, it will face secondary sanctions by the United States and Europe.

Germany is close to Russia with the Polish plain in between, and Britain is at Russia's gateway to the Atlantic Ocean. Thus, Germany and the UK are directly feeling the security threat from Russia. China is a distant country to Europe, but Russia is an existing threat. Besides, Russia and China are on the same page. The United States and Europe have become one with a common goal. The United States is finally able to stand by its allies.

2. Implications of the Ending of Europe-Russia Honeymoon

1) UK's Role in the Growth of the Russian Petroleum Industry

To understand the implications of European sanctions against Russia, it is necessary to understand the British-

Russian honeymoon relationship since the end of the Cold War in 1989. BP was at the center of it.

BP, the British oil giant with a long history became a company without oil fields after Middle Eastern countries like Iran and Iraq nationalized all of the company's assets in their countries without compensation in the 1970s. The North Sea oil field was owned by a state-owned British oil company and BP managed to merge with Arco and Amoco of the United States, but the future of the company without its own oil fields was bleak. BP's only hope was Russia that just crossed over the iron curtain and stepped out onto the world stage.

BP has been operating in Russia since 1990. At that time, Russia had provided 7% of the world's oil and one third of the global gas supplies, but its oil and gas production was on a decline due to lack of investment. The facilities were old and rusty and Russia's geological knowledge was rudimentary. BP first set up a chain of petrol stations in 1996, and bought a 10% stake ($751 million) in Sidanco owned by an Oligarch, Vladimir Potanin, in 1997. Two years later, Sidanco went bankrupt for some unknown reasons and merged with TNK owned by an oligarch Mikhail Friedman, but BP upped the ante instead. It acquired in 2002 a 15% stake in TNK and decided to form a 50:50 joint venture in the following year. Russia agreed to invest TNK and Sidanco's assets and BP to operate a chain of gas stations and invest 8 billion dollars in cash - the biggest foreign investment since Russia opened up its market. The deal was signed in London with British Prime Minister Tony Blair and Russian President Putin present.

Many Western oil companies, investment banks and oil traders followed the suit and rushed to Russia. ExxonMobil started drilling in Sakhalin in 2003 and began exporting oil in 2006. Shell also formed a $20 billion joint venture with Russia and started exporting oil in 2008.

The TNK-BP project was a huge success, but Putin was dissatisfied with it. The 50:50 joint venture without control in the oil industry that he promoted as the nation's growth engine was unacceptable to him. In 2011, TNK-BP voted for a share swap while working on the Arctic drilling project in partnership with Rosneft, Russia's top crude oil company led by an ally of President Putin, Igor Sechin. The decision would reduce TNK-BP to a minority stake in Rosneft. So BP took TNK to the International Court of Arbitration for violating the joint venture agreement, but BP's Moscow office was shut down and the Arctic drilling project had to see its partner changed to ExxonMobil. Clearly, it was Putin's plan to unify all oil businesses into state-owned Rosneft and natural gas business into Gazprom.

In 2013, in exchange for a 50% stake in TNK-BP, BP received $12 billion in cash and 18.5% of Rosneft shares. BP's CEO Bob Dudley hailed the deal, but others were surprised to see BP did not pull out all its stake and remain a minority shareholder with no controlling power over the state-owned company. This deal, though, was certainly lucrative. BP collected a total of $19 billion in dividends from the joint venture from 2003 to 2012. And during 2013-2021, the company received an additional $5 billion in dividends from Rosneft stock and was able to sell oil supplied by the Russian oil company.

In the aftermath of the 2014 Russia's annexation of Crimea, Western sanctions made further investment in Russia's oil business difficult, but BP had never considered to exit its stake in Rosneft until the outbreak of the war in Ukraine. The hefty dividends from Russia have become a source of funding for the British Pension Fund, and London has been a hub for Russian money and Russian oligarchs, earning it the nickname 'Londongrad'.

BP's 32 years of Russian business went down just three days after the Russia's invasion of Ukraine. After consulting with the UK government, BP announced it would dump the 19.75% stake it had held in Rosneft and warned it could lead to, in a worst case scenario, a $25 billion asset loss during the first quarter of 2022. However, there will probably be no asset reductions. The Bank of England has frozen the dollar reserves of the Russian central bank. If the worst scenario becomes true the BoE would compensate BP for the loss.

Shell, which became a British company last December, also announced the suspension of the Sakhalin-2 LNG development project with Gazprom. The company has a stake of 27.5% in the Sakhalin-II LNG facility, equivalent of 3 billion dollars. Sakhalin-2 produced a record volume of LNG in 2020, reaching 11.6 million tonnes, of which 3.2 million tonnes went to Shell, accounting for 10% of Shell's production. In the project, Japan's Mitsui and Mitsubishi are also partners. Shell also intends to end its involvement in the Nord Stream 2 pipeline project, in which it owns a 10% stake.

ExxonMobil withdrew from its joint venture with Rosneft in 2018 due to the 2014 financial sanctions against

Russia. However, it owns a 30% stake in the Sakhalin-1 oil and gas project and is doing business along with Indian and Japanese companies. Now ExxonMobile plans to discontinue operations at Sakhalin-1 as the US announced a ban on Russian oil imports to the United States. This means the days of U.K. and U.S. oil majors in Russia are over.

Meanwhile, France, a latecomer to the Russian oil and gas market is closely monitoring the situation. Total Energie still holds a 19.75% stake in Rosneft and is involved in two projects of the Yamal LNG with a 19.4% investment in the independent natural gas producer, Novatek. Russia accounted for 16% of the Total's oil and gas production in 2021 and paid a $1.5 billion dividend. Renault and Danon generate 9% and 6% of sales in Russia, respectively. France, a traditionally pro-Russian country is watching closely and waiting to see how the Ukraine crisis unfolds.

2) Germany, Biggest Customer of Russian Oil

It was U.K. that revitalized Russia's oil and gas industry and Germany was one of the biggest customer of Russian oil and gas as it does not have any oil major. Germany, an industrial powerhouse in Europe imports 60% of its energy, of which 55% of natural gas, 45% of coal, and 1/3 of oil comes from Russia.

Russia produces around 10 million barrels of crude oil per day and exports 7-8 million barrels, of which 4.3 million barrels are sent to Europe. If Europe is done with Russian energy, Russia can turn to China, but the maximum daily transport volume of oil pipelines linking Russian with China is only 500,000 barrels. Therefore, it will take years for China to replace Europe as the biggest customer of Russian oil.

To supply Europe with 4.3 million barrels of oil a day would require the United States and Saudi Arabia to increase their oil production and three oil giants - Iran, Venezuela and Nigeria - need to chip in. These countries are considered 'rogue states' by the United States, but the U.S. is making a reconciliation movement toward them after the Russia's war on Ukraine. However, since 2014, oil companies in the Middle East and the West have been pessimistic about the future for oil and gas industry and have not made additional investments, leaving only 4% of strategic petroleum production reserve. Oil facilities in Iran and Venezuela have also deteriorated without investment for over 20 years, so it will take time to further increase production. It is almost impossible to replace Russia in the short term, which accounts for about 10% of world oil production. Even if all of these oil-producing countries are combined, it will take 5 to 10 years to increase production. To drill and complete a shale oil well can take over six months and it takes another 6 months to transport it. Shale oil is a fundamental alternative, but the Biden administration is against it.

Still there are alternatives to Russian oil but gas is more difficult, and Germany, in particular, has no way out. The 2021 German consumption of natural gas was 102.1 bcm (billion cubic meter), which is comparable to the combined consumption of Italy 50.8 bcm, Britain 29.7 bcm, and France 25.7 bcm (total of the three countries 106.2 bcm). Britain could develop additional oil and gas fields in the North Sea area and has already built an LNG base off the west coast. However, Germany's dependence on Russian gas is difficult to break.

Today's German energy condition is the result of the Energiewende or great energy transition policy implemented for about 24 years during the reigns of Chancellor Gerhard Schröder and Angela Merkel. Merkel's center-right Christian Democratic Union has focused its Russian policy on "Change through Trade" succeeding Willy Brandt and Schröder of the Social Democrats. Their political belief that free trade would lead to international peace has now been neutralized by the war in Ukraine. Geopolitics always prevails.

Germany has to counter the energy crisis in the geopolitical reality, but the reality that Germany is now facing is not easy. Chancellor Merkel was aware of the problems of simultaneously pushing for nuclear phase-out and decarbonization. She believed a competitive natural gas commodity market would lower energy prices, citing "the market corrects the (wrong)[2] policy choice." So Germany did not sign long-term contracts of 10 to 20 years that most suppliers favored. Under the deal Germany can enjoy the benefits of price cuts in the period of oversupply, but it must have backup plans to guard itself against the tyranny of suppliers in case of an emergency.

Germany imports 55% of its gas from Russia and the rest from the Netherlands and the North Sea. Out of the total gas demand, 30% goes to power plants and 30%

---

2) The author inserted "wrong" in the quotation.

for businesses, and the remaining 40% for household cooking and heating. Of Russia's exports, gas accounts for 9% and oil for 45%. Oil export tax takes up 23% of the government's budget, while gas tax is only about 8%. Russia's economy is heavily dependent on oil exports but not as much as on gas. In other words, reduced gas supply won't hurt Russia much, but the German economy and households will scream.

In order to reduce dependence on Russian gas imports, Germany needs gas storage facilities and LNG regasification terminals. Rehden, a small rural town in northwestern Germany, has the largest natural gas storage facility in Western Europe. With an area of 91 football fields accounting for one fifth of Germany's gas storage capacity, it is owned by Gazprom. The Russia's largest state-owned gas company has influence over one third of gas storage facilities in Germany, Austria and the Netherlands.

LNG regasification facilities are spread across Western Europe including Spain, Italy, the west coast of England, the Netherlands, and Belgium. Even Poland and Lithuania have recently built LNG plants, but Germany has none. Spain has the largest LNG terminal in Western Europe which has a utilization rate of only 20%, but it is of no use to Germany because transporting the gas across the Pyrenees to Germany has been a problem. The Dutch and Belgian terminals are for their own use as the Groningen gas field edges closer to exhaustion. Germany has not made investments in gas storage facilities or LNG terminals. There are not enough number of LNG tankers. Germany is not ready to receive LNG.

Germany's lack of the gas infrastructure was caused by the EU's schizophrenic gas policy. Spain even opposed the "green" label for gas. EU has reclassified gas as a 'green transition fuel' in early 2022, but with lots of strings attached. In the face of repeated policy reversals no gas company would like to go for long-term contracts. No business would build gas storage facilities or LNG terminals under policy uncertainty.

Even when Gazprom cut gas supplies to Europe in the fall of 2021, British regulators opposed Shell's exploration and drilling of the North Sea gas field. Recent surge in electricity prices has rekindled discussions on gas field development. Europe has shown morbid repulsion toward fossil fuels saying they are 'dirty' energy.

Despite Prime Minister Scholz's move to fast track two LNG plants, it will take several years to complete them. There is a unprecedented interest in renewable energy, but it takes an average of six years to construct a wind turbine, including the process of obtaining permission from local residents. The construction of transmission lines connecting offshore wind farm in the German North Sea and the industrial south has been progressing, as expected, at a snail's pace.

Russia is confident that it can shrug off the Germany's decision to put the Nord Stream 2 gas project on hold for up to 10 years. Russia has been focusing on the development of the Bovanenkovo natural gas field that will be connected to the Nord Stream 2 pipeline. Other pipelines are connected to depleting gas fields. In the end, it is estimated Germany would eventually be left with no choice but to give in. Dmitry Medvedev, deputy chairman of Russia's Security Council said "Welcome to the brave new world where Europeans are very soon going to pay 2,000 euros for 1,000 cubic meters of natural gas." Russia holds the key to victory.

Europe has another option - fracking. A decade ago, Chevron, ExxonMobil, Shell and Total assessed European shale formations in hopes of replicating the US shale gas boom. According to a 2013 report Europe has shale gas reserves to be used for the next 60 years. Most of them are in the Eastern European region such as Ukraine, Poland, Romania, and Bulgaria, but France, the United Kingdom, the Netherlands, and Germany are also sitting on the shale formation. However, European governments succumbed to environmental protests and riots one after another. It remains to be seen where Europe's energy crisis will be headed in the face of a recurring energy war.

3. Sanctions on Russia May Cause the Formation of Financial Blocs

1) Future of Financial Sanctions on Russia

The U.S. and its allies shut off the Russian Central Bank's access to its $630 billion of foreign reserves. Most of them are held in the United States, Germany, France, United Kingdom, Austria and Japan, and China also holds 14% of Russian foreign reserves. Although China has not announced to freeze foreign reserves against Russia, it is hesitant to evade the financial sanctions in fear of a U.S.

secondary boycott. The Central Bank of Russia holds the fifth largest stockpile of gold in the world, with 2,299 tons of gold bars. Russia's National Wealth Fund (NWF) amounts to as much as $175 billion.

The seven Russian banks, including VTB, are excluded from SWIFT, a global dollar payments system. But Gazprombank is spared for handling energy payments. The EU has paid $70 billion for oil and gas in 2021. Russia's trade surplus in 2021 reached $19 billion. The financial artery of the world's 11th largest economy, with 800 billion dollars of foreign currency reserves and 70 billion dollars of crude oil payments every year, has been cut off.

Putin government, knowing the financial sanctions to follow as it had experienced after the annexation of Crimea in 2014 has been diversifying its foreign exchange reserves from dollars to euros, yuan, yen, and gold bars. This time, however, its foreign exchange reserves other than the dollar are cut off as well, leaving the world's third largest energy power in financial paralysis. It is unprecedented that one of the world's major economies is hit by the most severe sanctions ever.

Foreign exchange reserves are assets held by a central

bank at a cost to be used in times of crisis. Dollars and U.S. Treasury bonds are known as safe assets backed by the US government. Why would you have assets on reserve if you can't use it when you need it most? Gold bars stored in the vault of the Central Bank of Russia are useless as well. Who will lend money, taking them as collateral? Since 2000, the number of individuals and corporations subject to financial sanctions in the United States has increased more than tenfold, and now stands at 10,000. Financial institutions around the world are spending astronomical amounts of money to build a system to ascertain where they are subject to sanctions.

In the short term, the commodity markets stiffened and the Russian economy came to a standstill. Russia still produces Ural crude, but its financial market is not moving. Financial firms are not willing to issue LCs and do not buy Russian oil because they are afraid of public outrage and not sure of what will come next. Over the past decade, European financial institutions had been slapped with hefty penalties for bypassing U.S. sanctions on Iran. Logistics is also an issue. Access to the Black Sea was prohibited. Shipping giants Maersk and MSC have suspended Russia shipping. Everything from banks, ports, ships to merchants is frozen. Russian crude oil is sold at a discounted price of $18 a barrel with 70% of customers cut off. Will Russia be moving along a familiar path to international isolation as Cuba and Iran?

Russia can retaliate by shutting off the gas pipes. As mentioned earlier, natural gas accounts for only 9% of Russia's exports, but takes up 40% of Europe's energy sources and 55% of Germany's. Since 40% of the imported gas is for household uses, EU consumers won't be able to stand the gas crisis for long. In addition, Putin said Russia will only accept payments in rubles for gas deliveries to unfriendly countries. He added that Russia will deliver contractually agreed quantities. This means long-term contracts and Russia's gas will simply not get to commodity market. Europe now has to pay tens of billions of dollars' worth of precious Russian oil and gas in rubles.

It was the confidential pact between Saudi Arabia and U.S. Secretary of State Henry Kissinger (1975) that kept the dollar from falling down with the collapse of the Bretton Woods system in 1971 and the transition to today's system of floating exchange rates. Under the terms of the deal, the Saudis would agree to price all of their oil exports in US dollars exclusively and in return the U.S. agreed to protect the kingdom from outside aggression. The new 'oil standard' or the Petrodollar replacing the gold standard, had played a crucial role for the U.S. in maintaining the dollar as a reserve currency. All countries had to have dollars to buy oil. Saddam Hussein's decision that Iraq would switch from dollar to euro for oil trading led to the war in 2000, and Chavez, after announcing Venezuela would no longer accept dollars, was slapped with economic sanctions.

But Russia, which holds a tight grip on European energy markets, is different. The EU, classified as non-friendly entity, must either borrow money from the Russian central bank or export goods to earn the Russian currency. In the long list of economic sanctions, there are only a couple of cases that economic sanctions were effective - the Suez crisis and sanctions on Libya. Economic sanctions on Russia won't work.

2) Questions over the Dollar Payments System

If economic sanctions could stop Russia other than smaller and weaker countries like Cuba, Iran or North Korea, what would it mean? The more economic sanctions are employed, the more countries will try to avoid depending on the Western financial system. It would make threat of the sanctions less and less powerful.

Half of the world's $20 trillion of foreign exchange reserves and sovereign wealth funds are held by tyrannical nations. China knew from the War in Ukraine that its $3.3 trillion in foreign exchange could be suspended and that it could be kicked out of the Swift banking system overnight. India, too, feels that they are exposed to Western pressure. Countries under the threat of economic sanctions seek solidarity.

Over the past two decades, the United States have imposed economic sanctions on so many countries that has rather spurred them to move away from the dollar-centric financial system. The technological change of the financial markets in the coming decade will be an attempt to create a payment and settlement system that bypasses the Western financial system. It will eventually lead to reblocking of the global economy.

Then, could China's yuan be an alternative to the US dollar? China has 261 million of its digital currency users and its foreign exchange reserves of the Chinese renminbi are expected to rise from the current 2% to 7% in the next three to four years. China is working on CIPS, Cross-Border Interbank Payment System in Yuan, the Chinese equivalent of the globally-used SWIFT. But can China convince foreign governments to hold the renminbi? Now that the world can't trust the US government any more, can they trust the undemocratic China?

4. Conclusion

Russia is the 11th largest economy in the world, but it is a powerful player in the global raw material markets. In terms of production volume, it is the largest in gas, second largest in oil, and third largest in coal, and has a wide influence on the overall commodity market, including aluminum, copper, nickel, palladium, wheat and fertilizer. If economic sanctions on Russia are prolonged it will undeniably bring a shock to the global commodity markets.

Oil and gas became strategic commodities again. The EU, facing the tyranny of Russia, will show a major shift in its energy policy. In the meantime, the energy market will be moving away from being green-oriented and more competitive toward security and stability of energy supply.

There are three conflicting goals or Trilemma in energy policy - energy equity, environmental sustainability, and energy security which are colliding with each other. If Europe is to reduce its dependence on Russian gas, it will have to pay more for gas and make sacrifices in the fight against climate change. Geopolitics is pushing climate change away. The earth is slowly warming up, but the Ukrainan crisis is now boiling over.

The international financial market, established after the World War II, will also face a major turning point with the Russia-Ukraine conflict. The global financial markets will be split with a roar. It is not yet known which direction it will take. Russia, China, and sympathetic countries from the Middle East and South America will be joining the movement. Developing countries with large populations that hate Western pressure will also show a willingness to step in. The global economy may return to the bloc economies of the early 1900s.

Zbigniew Brzezinski, former national security adviser in the Carter administration wrote in his 1997 book, The Grand Chessboard. "The most dangerous scenario would be a grand coalition of China, Russia, and perhaps Iran, an 'antihegemonic' coalition united not by ideology but by complementary grievances." Let's watch closely what kind of world the war in Ukraine would create.

A New Solution for a New Cold War[1]

1. Drop in Oil Prices Ended the Cold War

It is widely known that it was neither a war nor a revolution, but the 'great plunge in oil prices' that brought an end to the Cold War that had been waged since 1945. After the 1979 Iranian Revolution, oil prices soared to nearly $40 per barrel, and oil exporting countries in the Middle East and the Soviet Union enjoyed a great economic boom.

U.S. President Ronald Reagan made a secret deal with Saudi Arabia to increase oil production in 1982, one year after his taking office in order to resolve the debilitating energy crisis. The U.S. needed Saudi Arabia to expel Iran which has declared anti-Americanism as a core pillar of its ideology from the global oil market and hit the Soviet economy which relies heavily on oil exports for up to 60 percent of its budget.

---

[1] This column was published on February 9, 2023.

The Saudi government had a good reason to welcome the partnership. As a young Kingdom with less political legitimacy and a smaller population in comparison with the populous and religious Iran, Saudi Arabia had been under continuous threat for its national security since its founding. Most of the threat came from the bitter territorial dispute with Iran over the Persian Gulf and the communist conspiracy in collusion with local tribes.

Drop in oil prices would be painful for Saudi Arabia as well, but it would deal a fatal blow to Iran which has a much larger population living on oil export revenues. Saudi Arabia thought falling oil prices would also hurt the Soviet Union that had been pulling the strings behind the scenes over the communists and then the market share of Saudi Arabia would go up straight, eventually putting itself on the dominant position in the Middle East. And there would be no more security problem. These are some of the reasons that Saudi Arabia hit the deal with the Reagan administration.

The oil price fell sharply in 1982 and remained at around $10 per barrel throughout the 1980s which, laid the groundwork for the Korean economic boom in late 1980s. And the Soviet economy, heavily dependent upon oil-for-money transactions with the West, suffered consistent shortages of consumer goods and finally collapsed in 1991. As British Prime Minister Thatcher put it, "without firing a single shot," the 46-year standoff between the U.S. and the Soviet Union came to an end.

2. Trump's New Cold War

Twenty six years after the end of the Cold War, however, "great-power competition" between U.S. and China began during the Trump administration (2017-2021). President Trump raged against globalization which lasted 26 years, criticizing that it shifted American manufacturing to China and destroyed the middle class by taking away blue-collar jobs and deepened economic inequality by increasing wealth of multinational corporations and the privileged few on Wall Street.

In fact, all the data backed this up. During the globalization era, US GDP grew to over $20 trillion, recording an average annual growth rate of 3%; New York Main Street, home to many large corporations and Wall

Street enjoyed record-breaking profits; and emerging US Big Tech and large media firms overwhelmed competitors in Europe and Asia. On the other hand, the share of middle class in the United States fell to 53% near the bottom among OECD countries; the public high school dropout rate was the highest at 30%; an increasing number of blue-collar workers went out of full-time employment and became gig workers who typically do short-term work for digital platforms.

Trump's solution to this was the 'America First' strategy. The US government talked multinational conglomerates into reshoring and encouraged shale oil companies to ramp up their drilling, turning the U.S. into a major exporter of oil and natural gas for the first time since World War II. Interest rates were slashed to boost corporate investment and increase in oil and gas production has helped to stabilize oil prices. When it comes to foreign policy, Trump administration scrapped or renegotiated free trade agreements and reduced US trade deficit with China by imposing a series of new tariffs on Chinese imports. President Trump's economic policies are characterized by **'low interest rates, low oil prices, high tariffs'**. However, Trump's presidency ended with defeat in the election after only one term in office and so did his policies.

3. New Solution to the New Cold War

Democratic President Joe Biden, who took office in January 2021, overturned all of Trump's policies, but made it clear that Trump's anti-China campaign would be kept alive. However, Biden's decision to revoke construction of the Keystone XL pipeline; suspend shale gas permitting on federal lands; and cut tariffs on China was hardly in line with the campaign. Now, one year after the outbreak of the Ukraine war and entering third year in power, the Biden administration's anti-China campaign is gradually taking shape.

1) High Oil Prices

Russia, one of the world's largest oil producers, has been imposed with sanctions in the international energy market following its invasion of Ukraine, which caused oil prices to skyrocket. Oil prices spiked immediately in the aftermath of the war to over $120 per barrel, which has led to global inflation, affecting all of the variables that define world economy. For now oil prices are stabilized at around $80 due to the shutdown of China's factories, but oil prices could surge again at any time.

Times have changed, but the oil market remains the same. The price elasticity of demand for crude oil in the short run is -0.06%. That is, demand decreases only by 0.06% for a 1% increase in price. On the other hand, the price elasticity of supply in the short run is +0.04%, and the elasticity of supply in the long run is +0.35%. This means that in the short term, supply increases by only 0.04% for a 1% increase in price, but supply increases by about 0.35% in the long term. As supply and demand in the oil market are inelastic relative to price, oil prices could, theoretically, rise up to 85% for a 5% supply shortage.

Russia produces 10 million barrels of crude oil per day, of which 6 million barrels are exported abroad. If Russia cuts oil production just 500,000 barrels a day, prices will go up sharply. When US strategic petroleum reserve reached its lowest level and OPEC refused to increase oil production, the US government reached out Venezuela in a bid to seek new sources of energy and sent Chevron executives to Caracas. But it would take years before Chevron can resume oil production in Venezuela.

Rising oil prices hurt oil-consuming countries, especially developing countries. The income elasticity of crude oil demand is close to 1.0, meaning that a 10% increase of income results in a 10% increase in oil consumption. Income elasticity varies depending on the level of development. Income elasticity of developed countries is only about 0.55 because they have few energy-intensive industries. On the other hand, that of developing countries is 1.1. Simply put, a 10% income rise brings about 5.5% increase in oil consumption in more affluent countries, but developing countries see 11% increase.

Unquestionably, the world's largest oil consuming countries are the United States with 19 million barrels per day and China with 12 million barrels per day. Japan consumes slightly over 4 million barrels a day, and Korea around 2.5 million barrels. Rising oil prices plague all these oil-consuming countries, but deals the hardest blow to China. It imports 8 million barrels of crude oil a day. If oil price rises by 10 dollars it will have to pay an additional $29.2 billion a year (8 million * 10 * 365). Korea will have to pay extra $9.1 billion.

The prices of basic industrial materials such as iron ore, coal, and copper that depend on imports and those of feed grains such as soybeans and corn for meat production are closely linked with oil prices. When oil prices rise, foreign currency spending on imports of these critical raw materials also rises vertically. Moreover, China, with its energy-intensive industrial structure, needs to import twice (1.1%) as much oil as developed countries (0.55%) to raise its economic growth rate by 1%. Surging oil prices are a nightmare for developing countries.

On the other hand, the U.S. and Europe have measures to mitigate the impact of rising oil prices. The US is both a consumer and producer of oil, and Europe is a home to oil majors like BP, Shell, Total, Eni and Equinor. To alleviate households' suffering from rising oil prices, the US and European governments can tax the windfall profits of oil companies. When 2022 settlement reports are out showing oil companies have made tens of billions of dollars of profits, the US and EU governments will impose an extra levy on these oil majors, and the tax revenue will go to energy subsidies for the poor.

Higher oil prices, in the meantime, make renewables attractive to investors. The Biden government and the EU Executive Committee are poised to promote renewable energy sources such as solar plants and wind farms. If oil prices drop and stay low, these businesses will have no choice but to rely on government subsidies. But when soaring oil prices take a big bite out of the profitability of fossil fuels, renewable energy businesses can operate on their own even when government subsidies are slashed.

Shortages in oil supply can cause oil prices to spike, and then it results in inflation. As long as the war in Ukraine does not end and as long as sanctions on Russian oil are not lifted, oil supplies could be disrupted anytime. This will strain the trade balance of all oil consuming countries, especially China, the world's largest oil importer.

2) High Interest Rates

Soaring oil prices caused inflation, and the Fed raised its benchmark interest rate to help curb inflation. The sudden interest rate hikes have led stock and property values to plunge and resulted in a strong dollar, also known as 'a super dollar' phenomenon worldwidely. Now that the exchange rate has stabilized, people expect that the Federal Reserve may pivot or reverse courses on its monetary policy only if inflation slows down. The bottom line, however, is that Fed's shift toward lowering interest rates seems like a far-off possibility.

Higher interest rates hurt even advanced economies, but they can devastate China. In the Chinese fiscal system, tax revenue is split between the central and local governments in a ratio of 75:25, which is called tax distribution system. Local governments, responsible for a range of vital services for people in defined areas, inevitably face severe budget shortfalls, which are often offset by land sales. Only half of the provincial government's budget is covered by tax revenue, so the remaining 50% has to be financed by selling physical properties like land. However, this would not work following the 2021 Evergrande liquidity crisis. China's local governments are under so much strains on their finances that they cannot even afford to pay for government employees.

Developing countries are in constant need of capital inflows and China is no exception. Foreign capital takes an essential part in resolving capital shortage. For this, China has relied on three major channels - the US stock market, European lending, and foreign direct investment.

The channel to the US stock market, however, was closed. The Trump government signed an executive order banning Chinese companies' access to Wall Street. In compliance with the order, the New York Stock Exchange delisted some of China's largest state-run companies including Huawei, and energy & telecom groups; restricted new

Chinese IPOs; and performed audit inspections on other US-listed companies. China's access to Wall Street investors money was put on a brake.

The main pillar of Europe's financial capital is the 'fixed income' market, i.e., 'bonds and loans'. China is the only resort that EU can turn to as European banks has been coming back to traditional banking after two decades of struggling to keep up with Wall Street. The EU, one of the largest capital markets in the world, has long been a linchpin of China's real estate sector. The Hong Kong financial market is dominated by European capitals mostly from Britain, Germany, France and Switzerland and their finance sectors have grown tapping on the opportunities provided by the Chinese real estate market.

It is impossible for the U.S. to impose regulations on the European banks as they are not under the US jurisdiction nor in the US market. The U.S. government may implement secondary boycotts against providing finance to China, but it cannot possibly stop European banks from providing mortgage loans to Chinese people who are so obsessed with buying property. But the Fed can raise interest rates.

The Chinese government has scrapped the 'three red-line policies', financial regulatory guidelines relating to the ratio of debt to cash, equity and assets, which was introduced to safeguard the property sector. In November 2022, for the first time since its economic reform and opening up policies, China's four major state-run banks began offering loans to property developers, and in January 2023, the mortgage interest rate for those buying a new apartment was down from 6% to 3%. Beijing is committed to the revival of the property market and European financial capital is set to take on a supporting role.

However, the Fed says it will raise rates to 5.25% by the end of 2023. If the FED's 'risk free' rate is 5.25%, how much should the interest rate be for the risky Chinese property sector loans? The FED is posing a question to European banks which will pay off better to invest in the Chinese property market or the US bond market. Now it is hard for Beijing to expect large reinforcements from Europe. The only viable option, now, is China's domestic banks. However, with local banks being already in rough shape Beijing has no choice but to rely on the four major state-run banks. This means that the People's Bank of China will print money as needed.

The Fed's raising interest rates will also weaken the

euro. The US dollar share of the world's foreign currency reserves accounted for more than 70% until the 1990s and now it has fallen to less than 60%. After the former Communist Bloc became involved in the global market, foreign exchange reserves around the world have been on the rise, triggering strong demand for dollars in the absolute term. But the euro, launched in 2000, has firmly established itself as the world's second most important international currency. The euro now accounts for 25% of world foreign exchange reserves, eroding the dollar's share.

What will happen if China and Russia, who have joined the anti-American front since the Ukraine war, continue to slash their demand for dollars? China's foreign exchange reserves are whopping $3 trillion, and Russia's $800 billion. China has already reduced its US Treasury holdings from $1.3 trillion to less than $1 trillion after Trump era. What would happen if these big players in the US Treasury market were to exit? America needs to be prepared for this.

EU countries with high ratios of government debt to GDP are groaning at the Fed interest rate hikes. It doesn't matter, though, to the fiscally conservative and economically strong northern European countries like

Germany and the Netherlands (so-called the Frugal North), but southern countries such as Spain, Italy, and Portugal whose government debt-to-GDP ratios exceed 120% and Eastern European developing countries suffering from capital shortages are crying out over the high interest rates.

Collapse of the euro won't happen. But southern and eastern European countries call for relaxation of EU fiscal rules, which may cause friction with northern European countries, and it could inflict damage on confidence in euro. Also, this would lead to an increase in demand for the US dollar. The US Treasury market may have new customers, even though losing China and Russia, from all over the world.

3) Low Tariffs

Currently the world economy is struggling under rising oil prices and high interest rates, and also intensifying inflation, so tariffs must be lowered. The Trump administration's introduction of a series of tariffs against China up to 25% proved a failure. Ironically, China's exports to the United States increased during the COVID-19 pandemic from 2020-2022 and the United States' trade deficit increased. Higher tariffs are passed on to consumers in the form of higher prices as the price of imported goods goes up.

President Biden signed the Inflation Reduction Act (IRA) into law and is pushing for reforms in the government purchasing of goods and services through revisions of the Government Procurement Reform Act. After completing policy adjustments to limit Chinese companies' access to the US market, the US government would drop some of tariffs against Chinese imports at the right time.

To sum up, the Trump administration's **'low oil price, low interest rate, high tariff'** policy is being replaced by the exact opposite **'high oil price, high interest rate, low tariff'** policy in the Biden era. In the 1980s, low oil prices plagued the Soviet Union during the Cold War. Time will tell whose policy will be more powerful in the new Cold War.

4. Korean Economy at Ease

Rising oil prices and high interest rates weigh heavily on the Korean economy as well. When oil prices go up, it hurts the trade balance of Korea that imports most of raw materials, eventually disrupting its supply and demand for foreign exchange. However, unlike the 1998 IMF crisis and the 2008 subprime crisis, Korea holds foreign currency assets of about $800 billion - $400 billion in foreign exchange reserves and $400 billion in overseas assets in the private sector - in the trade surplus accumulated over the last 2 decades. Korea is now recording current balance surplus. Korea has employed a very similar economic model to that of Japan, whose prime income comes from overseas investment in the forms of interest and dividends.

Higher interest rates put a burden on households and businesses, but the government sector whose debt-to-GDP ratio is around 50% can afford it. Unlike Europe, Korea's government finances are still sound, business activities remain dynamic and its job market is not in a bad shape. As long as the three main economic players - households, firms, and the government sector - are doing their jobs properly, Korea can defeat the current economic crisis only by stabilizing the property market that is currently reeling from high interest rates. As the real estate market is closely linked to the financial market, any disruption in the former may lead to disruption in the latter, which will inevitably bring negative impact on households and businesses. This is the reason why the government should play an active role in the restructuring of the real estate market.

After all, the biggest burden on the Korean economy is the US-China trade war. If the U.S. is decoupling from China, the future of the Korean economy straddling both the U.S. and China will be in turmoil. If the United States is pushing for a trade ban with China, numerous Korean companies doing business in China will be at the risk of huge losses. However, the U.S. is expected to continue its free trade stance with China while weighing China down on the macroeconomic front with "high oil prices and high interest rates." That is what the 'low tariff' policy toward China is all about.

In other words, as long as the US continues trade with China, there will be no major conflicts for the time being. Ultimately the U.S. will reduce trade with China, but it will continue to import goods in low-to-medium value-added products groups from China. This means that there will be no major changes in the trade structure between

Korea and China. Of course, Korea needs to reduce its dependence on trade with China in the long run.

So how long will this trend last? Higher interest rates place a great burden on the central government. The US government debt-to-GDP ratio is officially 120%, but some say it could be as high as 170%. The US government sector takes up about 37% of GDP, so if the debt ratio is around 120-170% and the government bond interest rate of 5.25% persists, it means that 17-24% of the national budget will have to be paid in interest only (120%/0.37×5.25%≒17%, 170%/0.37×5.25%≒24%). To be more specific, US taxpayers' hard-earned money will have to go to central banks around the world. Thus, higher interest rates are painful to the US government.

For that reason, the US government wants to lower interest rates as early as possible. Then when will the era of low interest rates come around? They blame the pressure from various economic variables such as oil prices, inflation, employment and wage growth, but the return to an era of cheap money depends on how the ongoing battle for global hegemony is unfolding.

Korean Economy Searching for Its Way Forward[1)]

1. Three Continents at a Crossroads

1) Rise and Fall of Regional Growth Rates

The economic growth rates of the US, EU and China were out lately. The US showed stronger growth in the first quarter of 2023 than expected, around 2%. On the other hand, the eurozone registered -0.1 percent growth and Germany, Europe's growth engine posted two consecutive quarters of negative GDP growth rates at -0.3% following -0.5% in Q4 2022. China, having reopened after ending most of its strict Covid restrictions in late 2022, recorded growth rate of 6.4% in Q2 2023, failing to meet the market expectation of 7%.

The US economy is booming, but the EU and China are at growing risk of slipping into deflation. It is the first time since the end of the Cold War that the EU and China show signs of synchronized economic downturn while the US

---

1) This column was published on July 31, 2023.

economy is booming. Is this a transitory phenomenon or a structural change?

Korea is an export-driven economy, exporting 70% of its products. It is vital for the Korean economy to predict economic fluctuations in the global market and assess regional development potentials. When three major economies of the world - United States, the EU, and China are blinking different signals, which lighthouse's signals should we follow to navigate through the hazy sea of global economy? Is the world economy shrinking or expanding? In this era of uncertainties, should the Korean economy be on the offensive or on the defensive?

2) Collapse of the Growth Formula in the Era of Globalization

With the end of the Cold War in 1991, the world economy became increasingly interconnected for the first time under the framework of WTO and it has become more tightly coupled for last 30 years. Despite the 1998 East Asian financial crisis, the 2008 Subprime Meltdown and the 2010 eurozone debt crisis, the world has evolved into a single 'global economy' going through its share of the booms and crises. When the U.S. economy faltered, it brought down East Asia as well, and when the eurozone fluctuated, Wall Street swang along.

The global economy has become one big organism. The US swept across the global market with the development of Internet and mobile revolution driven by innovative companies in Silicon Valley. Cheap products that would cater to deep-pocketed American consumers were made in China. Japan and Germany exported facilities and equipment to China, and later built huge factories in China. Japanese companies set up subsidiaries in China as the strong yen was squeezing their profit margins, while German companies advanced into the bigger Chinese market after they conquered the EU market.

Having been inundated with foreign capital, China was able to achieve rapid economic growth. Japanese companies rose from the excruciating 20 years of recession, beating the storm of strong yen with localization strategy. German companies have emerged as world champions in manufacturing. expanding their business beyond Europe to East Asia. Korea and Taiwan also joined the economic boom. Emerging resource powers such as Russia, Australia, and Brazil shipped raw materials to these countries. Everyone was getting richer.

Simply saying, prosperous America enriches China, which brings prosperity in Japan, Germany, Russia and Australia as well. What works here is an international division of labor - the US is in charge of innovation, finance, and consumption; Korea, Japan, Germany and Taiwan supply basic materials, intermediate goods and capital goods; and China assembles and sells them. China's working class, having taken part in the international division of labor for the first time out of their impoverished rural life, gradually joined the middle class and found themselves in the boon of another growth engine, the huge domestic market of China. The growth formula continued to work despite the fierce competition for supremacy between the US and China and the devastating COVID-19 pandemic, China's trade surplus with the US hit record high in 2022. However, now that the stringent lockdowns have been lifted in early 2023, this international division of labor model is on its way of dismantlement.

2. Continent on Edge, Europe

1) German Economy Melting Down

Negative growth in the EU is largely due to the downturn in Germany. As of the first quarter of 2023, Germany is the only G20 country to show negative growth. Manufacturing accounts for 20% of the German economy, and 10% of the German population, or 8.1 million people, are employed in manufacturing. Compared to the US and UK where manufacturing takes up for 10% and only 5% of the population are working in the industry, Germany is about twice the share. The stagnating German economy is the result of a manufacturing slump.

Undoubtedly, it stemmed from the Russian energy cutoff following the war in Ukraine. The halt in Russian oil supply at a lower price than the international rate deprived Germany of its only economic advantage, and the competitiveness of Germany companies nosedived. Despite the German government's relief package worth up to 200 billion euros to protect the embattled companies, German industrial production fell by 3.4% as of March 2023. Car production dropped by 6.5%, machinery and equipment by 3.4%, and construction by 4.6%. Exports decreased by 5.2% and retail sales in the domestic market also fell by 2.4%.

The problem is that this is just the beginning. Foreign orders declined significantly and Germany's energy-intensive industries such as automobiles, machinery, steel, and chemicals are halting production in response to the surge in energy prices. Although the German government announced to extend energy cost subsidies for two years, companies are well aware that the budget is not sustainable.

The German Socialist Party coalition government has declared a return to fiscal normality in 2024, ending the fiscal expansion of the past three years due to the COVID-19 pandemic and the war in Ukraine. The massive spending over the three years has brought the German government 507 billion euros of new debt and its debt-to-GDP ratio rose from 59.6% in 2019 to 67.7% in 2023, surpassing the 60% upper limit that Germany has set as a fiscal soundness indicator for EU countries.

Keeping EU leadership in hand is vital for Germany. For the unity of the EU and the stability of the eurozone, Germany is required to keep fiscal soundness and needs to become the most influential member state of the EU. Germany plans to cut the federal budget by 30.3 billion euros, or 9.4%, from 476 billion euros in 2023 to 445.7

billion euros in 2024. It will slash budgets on all sectors, except military spending. The cuts are indicative of Germany's strong will to take a leadership role in ensuring fiscal stability in Europe.

The high energy cost has been driving German companies to relocate abroad. In 2022 alone, foreign investment by German companies amounted to 135 billion euros, while foreign investment in Germany was only 10.5 billion euros, a whopping 13 times more outflow than inflow. A survey of 400 SMEs by the Federal Association of German Industry found that 16% of those already is moving parts of their production abroad, and 30% is preparing to.

70% of Germany's foreign investment goes to other European countries and the rest is mainly to the US and China. No doubt that the United States with a huge market and high growth rate is their main destination, but their investment in China has also been on the rise. Finance Minister Christian Lindner warns that the German economy is becoming too reliant on China and called for "de-risking" with China, but German companies are not listening.

In 2022, German's trade with China exceeded 300 billion euros, and German FDI in China reached 11.5 billion euros, totaling 114 billion euros in cumulative amount. VW, BMW, and M-Benz regard China as their biggest market, and BASF and Siemens have vowed to defend their market share in China. European officials taunt that German companies are decoupling with their own government. While economic policies are adrift, companies are relocating and unemployment is soaring up.

According to the national economic model, a country's GDP is composed of consumer spending, business investment, government spending, and net exports ($Y=C+I+G+Ex-Im$). As exports fall due to deteriorating profitability ($Ex \downarrow$), factories are shut down and move overseas ($I \downarrow$). As employment decreases, domestic demand also declines ($C \downarrow$). The government cuts spending to meet the debt ratio ($G \downarrow$). When consumption, investment, government spending and exports are all on the decline, this inevitably reduces GDP ($Y \downarrow$) - a fact too obvious to miss.

However, German government budget is still balanced, companies are in good financial shape, and household savings are large. So, there is no chance that the German economy will be in free fall. But it will be slowly melting down, like Japan's 'lost 20-year' slump.

2) Uneasy Europe

Germany and France, the two largest economies in EU, have been working together by coordinating their economic interests based on mutual trust. Germany whose economy is fueled by manufacturing, prioritizes free trade and stabilization of the euro, while France values greater autonomy in agricultural policies. The ECB has its primary goal to stabilize the euro and is under firm control by German officials from the Bundesbank which is well known for its inflation-averse monetary policy and France acquiesces in the German leadership within the ECB.

The ECB has been hesitant to pull the rate-hike trigger. When they finally raised interest rates, though started later than the FRB, the speed of hikes was not falling behind. They announced a rate increase to 3.75% in July 2023. Over the past three years, the financial soundness of governments around the world has deteriorated due to various spending spree such as temporary consumer subsidies for COVID-relief and energy subsidies. Nine EU member states including France, Italy, Spain, Greece and Belgium saw their debt exceed 100% of GDP. Rising interest rates have a major impact on the government budgets and financial markets of these countries.

Italy's right-wing government has issued a fierce criticism against the ECB decisions. With its debt ratio as high as 144% and manufacturing-intensive economic structure, Italy needs to keep interest rates low to ensure business vitality and financial market stability. Italian Finance Minister warns that any further hikes would be "senseless and harmful" and could lead to a recession.

Germany and Central Europe have been completely dependent on Russian energy, but the other countries are different. LNG is one of Spain's major energy sources, and southern France and Italy have been tapping on North African gas through the Trans Mediterranean Pipeline. These countries, furthermore, can do without Russian energy because their share of manufacturing is not large and they have stable inflation, good employment data and optimistic growth prospects. In June 2023, the Eurozone inflation rate fell to 5.6%, with Spain dropping to 1.6%, which was even less than the 2% inflation target. Italy also fell to 6.7%, the lowest since the outbreak of the Ukraine war. Unemployment rate in Eurozone also dropped to record-low 6.5%.

Then, will these countries want to raise interest rates? What will happen if a bank run occurs like in the SVB crisis in the US while trying to keep inflation under control by raising interest rates? Can the ECB guarantee unlimited amount of customer loans like the US Fed? Does Europe have a strong private financial company like J.P. Morgan to act as a knight in shining armor to save financial institutions from dreadful insolvency? In a hypothetical 'doomsday' economic scenario, the Fed predicted that the US banks still have more than enough capital to absorb losses even if they would lose $541 billion. Do European banks have the same capability?

European banks rely heavily on long-term bonds and loan products, which makes them more susceptible to rising interest rates. The ECB is forbidden by law from monetary financing, and Deutsche Bank and UBS are no longer healthy. As long-term bonds and commercial real estate suffer massive losses, European financial markets watch anxiously quarterly earnings reports from European banks. Investors are piling into cash and waiting for a hard landing of European financial market.

3. China's Economy in Free Fall

1) Features of the Chinese Domestic Market

It is almost impossible to make an meaningful assessment of the Chinese economy, the world's second largest and worth $17.8 trillion, based on largely opaque and inaccurate data. However, we can infer how the Chinese economy is faring based on economic theory.

As was mentioned earlier, a country's GDP consists of consumer consumption, business investment, government spending, and net exports (Y=C+I+G+Ex-Im). It is said that consumption accounts for only 40% of China's economy, worth 7.1 trillion dollars (approximately 5,100 dollars per capita). This is far below the average of 60% in developed countries. (e.g., up to 70% in the US). If China's consumer consumption reaches the average level of developed countries, its domestic market would be worth $10.7 trillion, which is $3.6 trillion larger than it is now. Citing this, the United States has been demanding that China should increase domestic consumption for the sake of the global economy.

What does it mean if Chinese consumers spend $3.6 trillion less? Household economics is similar all over the world. A significant chunk of household income goes to food, clothing and shelter, education, transportation and communication, and then the rest goes to high-end services such as industrial products and leisure. The Chinese people cannot go without daily essentials, so Chinese spending 20% less means that they do not purchase industrial products and high-end service goods. They are probably saving money to buy homes and deal with old-age insecurity. This is why China's household savings rate is so high.

Let's say that 70% of the $25 trillion U.S. economy goes to consumption, it would be $17.5 trillion. The consumption of 330 million Americans is $53,000 per capita, which is 10.4 times that of the Chinese. This means that there is a huge demand for industrial products and high-end services. China's domestic market is still falling short of expectations.

Demand for Chinese products basically comes from exports. China's trade dependence (sum of imports and exports divided by GDP) is nearly 35%, much higher than the US (20%). More problematic is the composition of imports and exports. While the US mainly exports raw materials and high-end service goods and imports final goods, China imports crude oil (about 250 billion dollars), food, raw materials such as iron ore (about 250 billion dollars), and electronic components such as semiconductors (about 250 billion dollars) and then processes or assembles to export them in return for dollars.

The United States procures the end products for its "already-existing" domestic market through imports and exports. The only thing you need is just to supply the products in a timely manner. On the other hand, China makes money by importing raw materials, processing and assembling them in factories, and then exporting them to advanced countries like the US and Europe. Exports are crucial in increasing jobs and income and creating a 'new' domestic market. Korea, Germany and Japan have a similar economic structure.

2) China's Economic Model in Trouble

China has been recording trade surplus of between 500 and 600 billion dollars every year since 2015. In 2022, it surged to 880 billion dollars, the highest ever-recorded with exports of 3.6 trillion dollars and imports of 2.7 trillion dollars. As exports were gaining steam, business vitality has become strong, employment has expanded, and the domestic market has grown. However, in the first half of 2023, the upbeat cycle was put to a halt.

China's share of US goods imports has consistently been more than 20% since the late 2010s, but plunged to 13% in the first half of 2023 when WHO declared an end to COVID-19. Mexico was the largest supplier of goods imports to the US, Canada the second, followed by Asian countries such as Japan, South Korea, and Vietnam. What does this mean? It means that US has been going thorough a major transformation for the three years of the pandemic to reconfigure their supply chains and diversify their import lines - namely, a shift away from China.

If exports to the US drop (Ex↓), the industrial capacity utilization rate in the Shanghai and Guangzhou will fall. Employment decreases and households cut back on spending (C↓). As economic vitality declines, investment also drops (I↓). Local governments, dependent on the central government funding, suffer budget crunch when real estate development projects are halted (G↓).

Foreign direct investment is the only thing that they can resort to, but its inflow is not fast enough. For example, officials from Zhejiang Province have made annual overseas trips over the past 20 years to attract foreign capital and last May they made their first European tour since the three-year COVID-19 epidemic. Wary of the friction with the United States, Chinese delegations sought to drum up European investment, but ended up with 'zero investment MOU' much to their dismay. The officials said that they didn't expect they would get cold-shouldered even by European investors.

Now the central government has to step in, but since 2015, China's foreign exchange reserves have not increased from the $3 trillion despite its annual trade surplus of $500 to $600 billion. Where did the money go? Hefty government funds went to "One Belt, One Road" initiative and "Made in China 2025," and they are almost impossible to recover now. There have been some achievements, though, in some industries, such as petrochemicals, electric vehicles, renewable energy and displays, but it is still not enough to lift China's economy out of the doldrums.

It is nothing but an illusion that China is self-sufficient with its huge domestic market even if exports fall. Chinese households are still poor and businesses are under constant financial pressure with debt ratios more than 300%. Debt-heavy local governments desperately need an injection of money from the central government, but the central government being at risk of running out reserves is equally frustrated. It is completely different from Germany, where households, businesses and governments are still sound. If the German economy is melting down, the Chinese economy is crashing. Then where is a way out for China, if any?

4. The US Economy on the Path to a Soft Landing

1) Vibrant US markets

The extent and speed of interest rate hikes by the U.S. Federal Reserve have taken the world by surprise and experts raised a concern that it could bring financial market instability and an economic recession. However, Federal Reserve chair Powell raised interest rates again at the July FOMC meeting, expressing his confidence that the US economy is in good shape and inflation will be under control. He also said that the Fed had no intention of lowering interest rates for the time being and more hikes are possible if they continue to get higher inflation reports.

What is the background of the Fed's monetary policy? It is that construction spending by US manufacturers is hitting unprecedented levels.

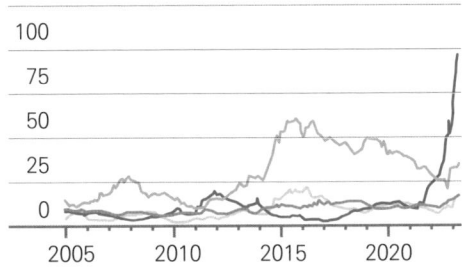

[Source: The Wall Street Journal, June 29, 2023]

In the aftermath of the 2008 subprime crisis, the "shale gas revolution" took place, and that has transformed the US from an oil importing country to a net exporter of petroleum. Major investments in the petrochemical industry were made in the mid-2010s amid oil prices on a downward spiral and growing supply glut.

Additionally, in the 2020s the US government unveiled a massive investment plan to rebuild the American supply chains following the end of the COVID-19 and for the hegemonic competition with China. The IRA and CHIPS Act are part of the plan and they are designed to provide incentives for renewable energy sectors such as semiconductors, electric vehicles, batteries, and solar power. In fact, the move has attracted Korean and Taiwanese chipmakers to the United States in a bid to receive tax benefits, and Intel, too, has come out with large investment plans to build new chipmaking factories. Petrochemical investment, which has been on hold for a while, is also on the rise. This is because many German chemical companies are moving their plants to the United States facing a prolonged energy crisis in Europe.

What is noteworthy is that investment plans announced by companies of electric vehicles, batteries, and renewable energy companies are yet to be implemented. Once the plans kick off, an investment boom comparable to that in the semiconductor industry will come around, and prices and wages will rise again. Then, Chair Jerome Powell may bring rate hikes on the table again.

As the federal government investment spending rises (G↑), investments by foreign companies from Korea, Japan, Taiwan, and Germany, not to mention US domestic companies go up (I↑). Job openings increases due to a rise in construction investment. So, it becomes increasingly difficult to recruit and retain production workers. Accordingly, wages and consumption rise (C↑). When consumption, government spending and investment increase together (C+I+G), the gross national product (Y↑) goes up. However, growing investment and consumption inevitably lead to increased imports, and this is the only factor that decreases the gross national product (Im↑, Ex-Im↓, => Y↓).

2) US Asset Market on Its Path Toward Soft Landing

The real economy is faring well despite soaring interest rates, but then how about asset market? The US economy has smooth sailing with the triple growth in government spending, business investment and consumer consumption. However, large amounts of assets locked in long-term bonds and real estate based on the assumption that low interest rates would last for a while, suffer from severe losses. In fact, three mid-tier banks in the US (SVB, First Republic, and Signature) have collapsed after a panic bank run amid liquidity worries.

The consensus view is that the next domino to fall is Commercial Real Estate (CRE). In downtown San Francisco, which was hit hard by the Silicon Valley recession, vacancies abound and shopping malls are closed down. In New York, the financial center of the world, land is more expensive than the buildings on it. Real estate investment funds sell their real estate at a 30% discount, being caught up in the wave of banking fear. One Liberty Plaza in Manhattan that Blackstone acquired at $1.55 billion in 2017, sold for $1 billion, and another Manhattan building Tower 56, which was worth $158 million back in 2008, was unloaded for $110 million in February 2023. Nearly $900 billion of commercial real estate loans are set to mature in 2 years and they are mostly variable interest rate and short-term loans. The eye of a typhoon is getting closer.

Meanwhile, SL Green, a REIT company sold a 49.9% stake in the 245 Park Avenue building in Manhattan to Japanese firm Mori Trust for $2 billion - the largest deal since interest rates began to rise in March 2022 and the price came close to $2.2 billion that China's Hainan Airlines

(HNA) Group had paid for the building. New York real estate market experts are closely watching. Is this a one-off deal or a sign of a resurgence?

In the past 30 years of prosperity, countries around the world have become rich, and financial institutions in Europe and East Asia are awash with cash. But when Europe is unstable and China is stagnant, where will they turn to? U.S. Treasury bonds can be an option, but it is terrifying to see U.S. banks go belly up after loading up on the long-term bonds.

Here looms New York real estate as a safe haven for European and East Asian funds. Real estate investments can be a good long-term cash cow as long as original tenants are financially stable and sound. Prices may go down in the short term, but if the US economy remains healthy, the value of New York real estate will eventually rebound in the medium to long term. If a strong dollar comes around due to stagnation in Europe and China, you may get foreign exchange gains as well. Mori Trust may be betting on a weak yen when everyone expects the yen's recovery. For foreign investors, New York real estate is emerging as a "store of value" that will replace US Treasury bonds. Fund inflow from Europe and East Asia could deliver a soft landing for the US asset market.

5. Conclusion – Piggyback on the US Economy

All of these combined explains the recent changes in the Korean economy. Over the past year and a half, the trade balance deficit, which was a major concern of the Korean economy, due to the sharp decline in the semiconductor industry and decreasing exports to China, has turned to a surplus. Exports to the US are on the rise, offsetting the decline in exports to China. Semiconductors and petrochemicals are struggling, but automobiles, machinery, shipbuilding, and renewable energy sectors are seeing exports increase and profitability improve. Since the NATO Madrid meeting in June 2022, remarkable achievements have been made in the defense sector as well. Domestic investments continue to be made in the semiconductor, electric vehicle, and battery market. Above all, the labor market is clearly not bad even though construction industry is struggling.

In this context, the Korean economy grew 0.6% in the

second quarter following 0.3% in the first quarter of 2023. Exports fell only by 1.8%, thanks to strong performance of the Southeast Coastal Industrial Belt offsetting the sluggish semiconductor industry. In the meantime, imports decreased further due to falling oil prices (-4.2%), turning the trade balance into a surplus (net exports contributing to GDP, +1.3%). Housing construction was put on halt following the PF crisis or real estate project financing crisis (construction industry, -3.4%), but manufacturing facility investment in new industries alleviated the losses (construction investment, -0.3%; facility investment, -0.2%). Most importantly, job market is not bad, so domestic consumption is holding up. (-0.1%). The Bank of Korea says that the Korean economy is projected to grow by about 2% in the year of 2023. Plummeting semiconductor prices, shrinking trade with China, and the crippling construction industry would mean a perfect formula for a perfect storm, but the Korean economy is still in good shape.

The key to future success is now clear. There is no need to screen trading partners when it comes to running an economy, but it is crystal clear which of the three continents; the United States, Europe, and China for Korea to put more weight on. Korea needs to expand exports or advance to the US market or advance into Mexico and Canada, which share borders with the United States and are reinforcing their supply chain links with the US. In particular, Mexico is close to the newly emerging industrial zone in the southern United States and has cheap labor forces, thus is very likely to rise as the most the attractive investment destination for Korean companies. And then Alternative Asia or Altasia including India, Vietnam, and Indonesia with growing exports to the US will be the next. May Korean companies wisely deal with increasing geopolitical risks and bravely move forward amid growing economic uncertainties.

Nationalization of China's Real Estate Sector and Europe's Role[1]

1. Corporate structure of the Chinese economy

The vast size of China's economy and its complex industrial networks with their statistics so opaque, make it difficult to see through what is really going on in the country. The stunning high-tech industrial zones in Shenzhen and Shanghai leave us in awe, but the contrasting backwardness in the western inland of China takes us by surprise.

Inarguably, China's strong economic growth has been hauled by manufacturing industry which is made up of numerous businesses. In the past, China's manufacturing industry mostly consisted of state-owned enterprises and TVEs - township and village enterprises. Later economic reforms and opening-up have enabled China to attract a

---

[1] This column was published on May 20, 2024.

large number of joint ventures with foreign investors and they have become leading exporters. Now in the 2020s, however, the global economic players from China have again become domestic brand conglomerates.

Big boys are found in both state-owned and private enterprises in China. Almost all of the country's key industries, like steel, petrochemicals, automobiles, communications, and resource development, comprise state-owned enterprises. Platform companies such as Alibaba, Tencent, and JD, which started out as tech companies but have now been promoted to a part of social infrastructure, were once private companies with a market value of hundreds of billions of dollars on the New York Stock Exchange, but after the Beijing government's sweeping regulatory measures, they came under the government's tight grip.

Most of China's global market players, in the meantime, are private companies. BYD and Nio in electric vehicles; CATL, the world's No. 1 battery manufacturer; Huawei, TCL, and Hisense in electrical and electronics; Oppo, Vivo and Xiaomi in mobile phones; SMIC in foundries, and many solar and wind turbine companies are private companies, at least on the surface. These Chinese companies are taken as a threat to foreign governments and competitors in the global market as they have come up with inexpensive and innovative products. Albeit being private companies, they are all beneficiaries of government subsidies as part of 'Made in China 2025', an initiative to comprehensively upgrade Chinese industry.

In line with them are real estate firms, approximately accounting for 30% of the Chinese economy. Some are private companies such as Hengda (*hereafter* Evergrande) and Biguiyuan (*hereafter* Country Garden) and the others are public companies owned by local governments. The real estate industry has been responsible for 90% of China's fixed asset investment and 50% of economic growth in the 2010s. China's property market has been a key driver of its double-digit growth in the 2010s. Tapping China's middle-class dream of homeownership, China's property developers had been thriving with financial support from regional banks owned by local governments and Hong Kong's LGFVs (Local Government Financing Vehicles, or special-purpose state-owned enterprises designed to help local governments have access to other sources of liquidity other than direct borrowing by governments). However, China's real estate boom was put on hold when the

Evergrande crisis broke out in 2021.

2. What China needs to do for its economic recovery

As the real estate industry accounting for 30% of China's economy and 50% of its growth comes to a standstill, the economic growth rate accordingly plummeted to 5%, half of the double digits in the 2010s. Many economists argue that Chinese economy has transformed into one driven by domestic demand and it is crucial to promote domestic consumption to resolve the current crisis. In a bid to boost flagging economic growth with domestic demand, the Chinese government launched a trade-in plan, also known as Refurbishing Program in which subsidies will be offered to Chinese consumers who replace their old TVs and refrigerators with new models.

However, will it be any good turning to domestic demand in the society with its per capita income of just $13,000? Consumers should first spend their income on essential consumer goods such as food, clothing, shelter, transportation, communication, education and leisure, and then use the remainder on industrial products. Compared to consumers in developed countries with the income level of $30,000 or more, Chinese consumers earning $13,000 per capita have significantly less spending power on industrial goods.

Once China's consumption accounted for about 60% of the gross national product (GNP), now it has plummeted to around 40%. Some say this is because Chinese consumers have opted for precautionary saving over consumption in the face of uncertainty about the Chinese economy in the future. What kind of change have Chinese consumers gone through in the past 5 years?

The 20% decline in consumption in just five years mainly stemmed from the real estate slump. In lower-income economies, the housing market has a profuse influence over demand for industrial products. A house is, in fact, a huge collection of industrial products such as cement, rebar, aluminum, glass, wood, pipes, wires, etc. Furthermore, the purchase of new homes leads to the demand for various furniture, home appliances, kitchenware and bathroom accessories. And then it will gradually extend to the so-called luxury goods such as cars and luxury accessories as the homeowners aspire to blend in the newly-joined upscale community.

As China's property market has reached a stalemate, construction is delayed and the decrease in demand for building materials hits hard the companies dealing in construction materials such as steel, cement, and glass. Even worse, delayed occupancy of new homes results in decline in demand for home appliances, furniture, and home accessories, and in turn the sale of automobiles and luxury goods also decreases. The drop in domestic consumption does not mean that consumers are holding back on essential spending but the demand for the industrial products has fallen headlong. In order to get its economy back on track, the Chinese government has no choice but to rescue its crisis-hit property sector.

3. What should be done to normalize the real estate sector

Cash-strapped local governments in China have been boosting their revenues by selling swaths of land since the 1994 Fiscal Reform implemented in the early years of President Jiang Zemin. Chinese real estate developers have acquired land and expanded their business aggressively taking on bank loans from local governments and bonds issued by Hong Kong LGFVs.

Property giant Evergrande has filed for bankruptcy, after its failure to expand its business into unexperienced areas including electric vehicles, and Country Garden, one of China's biggest homebuilders, though having committed to its core construction business alone, was also declared default on its debt after the number of unsold new homes increased in large-scale housing projects. Facing a major financial squeeze, many Chinese real estate developers are at risk of going down the same road.

Generally, the main source of finance for Chinese real estate developers is local banks and Hong Kong's LGFV. The "Big Four" state-owned banks, Industrial and Commercial Bank of China (ICBC), Bank of China (BOC), China Construction Bank (CCB), and Agricultural Bank of China (ABC) do not lend to the real estate companies. If the real estate market turns downward, local banks become insolvent, facing a chain reaction of defaults to sweep the banking industry as well.

Hong Kong's LGFVs, of which European banks are the

main shareholders, can no longer finance real estate developers. Collateral value has fallen by more than 30%, and there are a large number of unsold and vacant houses. Now that it is impossible to collect interest payments on the existing bonds, getting new loans is out of the question. It is widely known that French banks are the biggest investors, apart from British, German and Swiss banks.

With the property rights of the entire population at stake, should the real estate crisis be left to the market's self-regulation? It will eventually give rise to a series of bankruptcies of real estate companies, and a majority of Chinese people will be left with huge financial losses and unfinished apartments. This is bound to lead to political instability. The promises made to those who bought pre-sale homes must be fulfilled no matter what. This is not just an economic problem, but a political problem. What is the solution?

4. Nationalization of Chinese real estate sector and Europe's role

The first step for insolvent real estate firms to get back on their feet is debt restructuring and new loans. Private shareholders' rights will be abrogated, loans from local banks will be converted into equity, and private developers will come into the possession of local banks.

However, local banks are heavily exposed to bad property loans, so they are not capable of providing additional financial support to the embattled developers. Local banks can only turn to the state-owned banks. The Chinese government was planning to merge "bad banks" with the state-owned banks or take them over. This will kick off a process in which state-owned banks take control of local banks and then local banks make indebted property developers their subsidiaries (namely, nationalized companies). Ultimately, China's real estate sector will go through nationalization over the years.

But there is a catch – what happens to the LGFV debt, which has ballooned to trillions of dollars? The local governments have before come to rescue, offering de facto guarantees for LGFV debts. But who would underwrite bonds issued by the local governments that are apparently teetering dangerously close to bankruptcy? Wouldn't it be a better idea to turn its back on foreign debts, go through legal procedures, and write them off?

Writing off the local government debt, though, means that China is breaking up with Europe. Europe's financial sector, heavily based on fixed income assets such as long-term bonds and real estate finance, has been struggling with the interest rates hike that started in 2022. A Collapse of the LGFV bond market could drag down European banks and pension funds, inflicting colossal losses. And its consequences could be much bigger than we can imagine – not just restructuring of financial institutions, but to the point of shaking the European banking system. And that could escalate into diplomatic dispute between China and European countries.

Now it's time China's central government step into the ring, but it is already busy with the Belt and Road Initiative, Made in China 2025, and the arms race with the United States. The Chinese state-owned banks, which are mandated to support the government's economic agenda, are in bad shape as well. If the central bank prints more money to resolve debt problem, it could ignite inflation by triggering liquidity evaporation. There is no other option left for Beijing other than issuing special long-term bonds, but with the United States keeping it in check, who would purchase China's special-purpose bonds?

Here lies Europe's role in China's debt crisis. It has become obvious that European financial institutions cannot take repayment of bonds that they bought from Chinese local governments through the LGFVs in Hong Kong. If Beijing issues central government bonds and provides liquidity to debt-ridden local governments, European financial institutions can at least recover money tied up in LGFVs. To that end, however, European financial institutions have to underwrite Chinese government bonds, but it is better than crushing defaults. It would be even better if Beijing pledges to repurchase the long-term bonds a few years later just as the ECB did during the Greek debt crisis. The European central bank had pledged to buy up Greek government bonds by way of establishing external financial organizations in 3 years under its unlimited buy back scheme, to bail out French banks which had purchased the Greece bonds in 2011.

5. Significance of China-France relations

The trade ties between China and France have traditionally been weak. China's transaction with France mostly comes in the form of Chinese middle class consumers buying luxury French brands including wine, cosmetics and accessories, and millions of Chinese tourists visiting France. In terms of trade relationships, China is the buyer and France is the seller. Critics say that President Xi Jinping has, actually, no industry agenda to discuss with President Macron.

When it comes to finance, however, the tables are turned. France has long been suppliers of funds to China. President Xi chose France as his first destination for his European tour in five years in early May 2024. What was his state visit to France for?

It is no coincidence that on May 13, right after President Xi Jinping returned from his visit to France, China's Ministry of Finance unveiled plans to issue government bonds worth 1 trillion yuan, about $140 billion. China issues first batch of 30-year stimulus bonds or even 50-year ultralong bonds at yield of 2.5-2.6%, in contrast with the interest rate on a 10-year U. S. Treasury bond at 5.25-

5.5%. The Chinese bonds are not likely high in demand under ordinary circumstances. But it will be OK if China and France have promised to cooperate. France has addressed the Greek debt crisis in a similar way.

Excluding local government debts, the fiscal situation of the Chinese central government remains sound, with a debt-to-GDP ratio of around 20%. If Beijing issues government bonds and succeeds in attracting foreign investment to repay the debts of local governments and LGFVs, European financial institutions will not have to face substantial losses. In short, highly indebted Local governments will see their default risk lowered and the central government take over their debt, and European financial institutions will end up holding China's government bonds which will generally offer stable yields.

Property developers will resume construction and citizens can move in their new apartments. The Chinese government, accredited with saving its crisis-hit property sector may see a rise in public support, and the revitalized real estate sector will once again be the driver of the nation's economic growth. An increase in the rate of economic growth means higher GDP, which will in turn lower the government debt ratio. The government debts may not be repaid but reissued. But as long as interest payments are made without a hitch and increased volume of China's government bond issuance enables the number of market participants to grow, there will be no complaints. As for the European financial companies, China's participating in sovereign bond means an opening of the world's second largest bond market following the U.S. Treasury market. Everyone will be happy.

6. Nationalization of the Chinese economy in the final phase

It should be noted that nationalization of China's economy will be completed through this process. In fact, restructuring the massive real estate industry all at once is extremely risky. However, stabilizing the crisis-hit property sector with European financial capital chipping in, China's goal may be within reach.

If it is successful, Beijing will gain bigger control over local governments. The era of decentralization of power to local governments that began under Deng Xiaoping's leadership comes to an end, and local governments are increasingly falling under the full rein of the central government. Chinese local banks, which have been a main source of finance and power for local governments are going down the road to becoming dominated by the four major state-owned banks.

The real estate sector, which once accounted for as much as 30% of economy, will gradually come under the control of the central government. China's $18 trillion economy will have only a handful of enterprises off leash. Platform companies, tech companies, real estate firms, and local banks will be nationalized. The only remaining private enterprises will be those in the sectors of electric and electronics, semiconductor, and electric vehicles along the southeastern coast. Concentrated in Shenzhen and Shanghai, these companies are main driving forces of innovation and creativity in the Chinese economy, so it is preferable to keep them private. However, even these companies cannot completely be untainted by government subsidies in their bid to succeed in the fiercely competitive international market.

This brings to an end the journey toward capitalism that China embarked on over 40 years ago under the banner of reform and opening up. And what is known as "the state advances, the private sector retreats" (國進民退), or more bluntly, the "nationalization of the means of production," is essentially completed. That is to say, centralization of the Chinese economy is being realized at a stage where its production capacity is much more advanced than that of the former Soviet Union.

Will this process proceed as planned? Will European countries, calling for de-risking them from China, cooperate in this process? Will the United States tolerate the financial collusion between China and Europe? It remains to be seen how the China's issuance of special government bonds will impact the international financial market and the Chinese economy.

Implications of the Financial Blockade against China and the Onset of Monetary Easing[1)]

1. Financial Coupling of US and China

In March 2023, the White House was considering sending envoys to Wall Street. Their mission would be to advise U.S. financial institutions not to buy stocks and bonds of Chinese companies, and to figure out measures to counter China in the years to come.

In the process of the preliminary survey, however, the White House learned that U.S. financial institutions' portfolio investment in China had already fallen to the lowest level. Facing geopolitical concerns, Wall Street has put a 'sell' on its China holdings and many financial institutions pulled out of China. Hence, the U.S. government's plan to dispatch envoys was scrapped.

As was the case during Korea's economic development

---

1) This column was published on September 19, 2024.

when foreign loans were desperately needed, overseas funds are one of the most crucial factors for economic growth. Since the 1990s, Wall Street has been the lifeline for China's record economic growth and the New York Stock Exchange has made a substantial contribution as well. Chinese telecommunication companies were among the first Chinese companies to be listed on the NYSE as they were expected to show an explosive growth in the country with a population of over 1.4 billion. And they were followed by China Mobile in 1997, China Unicom in 1999, and China Life Insurance (中國人壽) and PetroChina in 2000.

China's state-owned enterprises (SOEs) in energy, petrochemicals, nonferrous metals, and finance flocked to New York. Wall Street didn't care whether they were owned by the People's Liberation Army, the central or local governments, or the princelings. As long as they had a profit model and were monopolies, they were received with open arms. Big investment banks such as J.P. Morgan, Merrill Lynch, and Goldman Sachs led U.S. investors plowing billions of U.S. dollars into the Chinese firms.

New players entered the arena; they were private equity firms (PEFs) that raise capital from institutional investors including pension funds and operate investment funds. Blackstone, KKR, and Carlyle, for instance, invested in emerging Chinese tech giants like Tencent, Baidu, and JD.com in hopes to emulate SoftBank's phenomenal success in investing in Alibaba. These PEFs paid off with higher returns to investors weary of the Fed's policy to keep its benchmark interest rate low in a bid to overcome the 2008 financial crisis. Chinese companies were the goose laying the golden eggs, and China was a new El Dorado.

The Chinese firms to which PEFs were committed were attractive investments for pension funds. They had little chance of going bankrupt, and the investment outlook was bright with significant size of the investment and de facto monopoly status. These companies grew vigorously with private equity investment, and the pension funds enjoyed decent profits. Following the great success of those tech companies, more Chinese companies lined up for U.S. IPOs at the NYSE with new business models. The private equity sector has gotten so enormous that it has become another pillar of Wall Street.

Nouveaux riches crowded both continents across the Pacific. The scars of the 2008 subprime crisis and the 2011 European financial crisis were nowhere to be found, and the financial power of the United States had become stronger, to reach a supreme position where it commanded 70% of the global financial market.

2. Prelude to Financial Blockade against China

Even when Trump launched a trade war against China after coming to power, it was hard to imagine that U.S. financial institutions split with China. It has been criticized that Germany and Japan have maintained strong industrial ties with China, but it was widely known in the financial world that the U.S. had been the main source of foreign capital for China, and China was a major investee for U.S. firms. Trump's anti-China policy sent shudders throughout Wall Street, a wave of panic gripping investors. What should they do with all the enormous amount of money they had put in the Chinese companies?

Nearing the end of his term, in November 2020 President Trump signed an executive order, delisting 31 Chinese state-owned telecommunications, energy, and technology companies from NYSE on the ground that these companies were suspected to have been controlled by the Chinese People's Liberation Army.

The Chinese companies were surprised by the order, but Wall Street was flabbergasted. The Washington's move left the portfolios of asset management companies in ruins overnight, and institutional investors with significant China exposure were floundering in bewilderment and chaos. Trump proved that he was committed to going tough on China by removing China's three major state-run telecommunications companies - China Mobile, China Unicom, and China Telecom - from the New York Stock Exchange between January 7 to 11, 2021, right before the end of his term.

Soon after, on March 26 tremor began to break out with the downfall of Archegos Capital. This triggered a massive sell-off at the stock market as Goldman Sachs and other Wall Street heavyweights quickly moved on liquidating their assets tied to Archegos such as Baidu and Tencent; VIPshop, one of China's largest discount retailers; iQIYI and GSX Techedu, leading Chinese online education video streaming sites; and ViacomCBS and Discovery, which were U.S.-headquartered multinational mass media companies. The primary cause of the brutal stock market crash was Archegos' failure to meet the margin calls in CFDs (Contracts for Difference).

Bill Hwang, the founder of Archegos Capital Management, was a veteran investor who had earned reputation with his own hedge fund, Tiger Asia Management. He turned Tiger Asia into a family office, renaming it Archegos Capital Management. A family office is a privately held company that handles investment management and wealth management for a wealthy family or tycoons. And he invested heavily in CFDs of Chinese tech giants.

A CFD allows traders to speculate on the future market movements of undervalued stocks without actually owning the stocks. Bill Hwang, overconfident in the rise of Chinese Big Tech stocks, had bet big on risky investments and amassed one of the world's greatest fortunes, but it was wiped out in a blink when Trump issued the executive order.

Archegos was reported to have borrowed around $10 billion from Wall Street investment banks to enter into CFD instruments. Nomura announced a loss of $2 billion in trades it had put on for the hedge fund, and Credit Suisse was estimated to have suffered a loss of over $5 billion.

It is noteworthy that Japanese and Swiss capital took the biggest toll among Wall Street banks in the Archegos disaster.

Despite its sweeping overhaul of business changing CEOs several times over the past 10 years since the subprime crisis, Credit Suisse was not able to withstand the final blow from Archegos and marked the final chapter in the 168-year-old bank's history in 2023. The collapse of Archegos was an event that heralded the beginning of the U.S.-China financial decoupling.

3. Completion of Financial Blockade

Wall Street expected a less-blunt, more tactful financial policy toward China from the Biden administration, but things didn't unfold the way they wished. About a year after taking office, the Biden administration's policy toward China finally took shape. The three major Chinese oil companies- PetroChina, Sinopec, CNOOC- and China Life Insurance and Aluminum China, were forced to delist from NYSE in 2022 amid growing regulatory demands.

The rest of the story is well known. Chinese companies had to either move to the Hong Kong or the Shanghai exchanges, or comply with the U.S. regulatory demands to open their books for audits in order to avoid delisting risk. IPO process for new Chinese companies has become more complicated, and the China's securities regulator encouraged the nation's companies to list in Hong Kong or Shanghai. Several big names including Baidu and Tencent went public on the Hong Kong stock exchange, and Didi Chuxing, China's biggest ride-hailing firm, said in 2021 that it withdrew the plan to list at NYSE and issued its shares in Hong Kong in compliance with the government's policy. Stricter regulations on video game and online education companies have been overused, and the much-anticipated listing of fintech giant Ant Group was suspended, dealing a blow to its billionaire founder Jack Ma.

Moreover, China experienced a significant pullback of U.S. private equity investment. The PE firms which had 30 investment deals closed in 2021 alone at the beginning of the Biden administration, decreased the flow of capital investments to a trickle, in the face of growing geopolitical tensions and China's new stock market regulations. The Fed's interest rate hike also played a role, drastically slowing down the flow of capital from pension funds to private equity funds.

In 2024, seven of the top 10 private equity firms have made no new investment at all, and only 5 transactions – mostly small[2] – were made by the other 3 companies. The 28 years of China's 'gold rush' since 1997 have now come to an end.

Investment banks and private equity firms – two major vehicles of wealth creation in Wall Street have made almost 'zero' portfolio investment and buyout equity investment over the 8 years under the Trump and Biden administrations. European commercial bank-led collateral loans for Chinese property developers in the form of LGFVs (Local Government Financing Vehicles) also halted following the Fed's interest rate hikes starting in March 2022. The implausible financial decoupling between the West and China is now moving closer towards completion.

---

2) See the front page of the Financial Times, August 26, 2024

4. Implications of the Financial Blockade

Unlike the autocracy society that operates under the control and order from the top, a market economy relies on incentives to induce persistent participation. In order to end the era of Chimerica (a compound formed from China + America) that lasted for three decades and to successfully implement its policy of blocking China, Washington must 'decouple' from China. To that end, industrial, technological, and financial blockade is the key.

Industrial and technological blockade is relatively easy to impose, for it targets business companies having no voting rights. Some of the most powerful weapons that the U.S. government has been wielding for the blockade are the Inflation Reduction Act (IRA), the Chips and Science Act, and tariff increases. Financial blockade, however, is self-destructive because it hits the assets of individual investors. When investors' wealth evaporates as a result of the government's financial control, voters will most likely turn their backs in the upcoming elections. Investors are voters and voters decide election results.

In the column published in February 2023, *"A New Solution for a New Cold War"*, I pointed out that the Fed's interest rate hikes would directly hit the Chinese economy, which is already saddled with a crushing debt hangover. Further, the executive orders and follow-up measures issued over the past eight years enabled the U.S. financial industry to be separated from China's.

Despite concerns, there was no stock market crash or financial panic. The damage to financial institutions was limited to Credit Suisse and three U.S. regional banks going down. Now, the final step for the financial blockade is finetuning of legal and regulatory systems.

On September 18, 2024, the Federal Reserve lowered interest rates, easing monetary policy for the first time in two and a half years. It might have resulted from slowing inflation, but was also synchronous with the financial blockade against China that has been in place for the past eight years. Now the market conditions are prepared for interest rate cuts as higher interest rates increase governments' fiscal vulnerability in both the U.S. and Europe and undermine economic stability of its allies. Global investors are losing appetite for China.

As for China, it must continue to import food, crude oil, raw materials and capital goods for survival and economic development of the nation, for which a stable supply of foreign currency is required. There are two sources of foreign currency supply, the first being capital market by means of stock and bond sales, bank loans, foreign direct investment, and the second being real economy - net exports (total exports minus total imports). China has already suffered plummeting foreign direct investment for several years, and now it is denied access to capital markets of the United States and Europe, how will China be able to raise capital for its future economic growth?

Export is the last card left for China. Recent gust of oversupply in steel and petrochemical industry is a foreboding harbinger. In the international trade market, price is the sole determinant of demand for these intermediate goods. This is why the United States imposed high tariffs on steel and aluminum imports from China.

The Chinese government, in desperate need of foreign currency, will provide subsidies to companies that produce intermediate goods and flood global markets with whatever goods exportable such as steel, nonferrous metals, petrochemicals, textiles, glass, construction materials, machinery & electronic components. China's industrial capacity utilization rate, either in state-run or private sector, will be kept high, no matter how much losses they make. For Beijing fears more the potential social unrest fueled by unemployment than corporate losses.

When the international market is inundated with cheap Chinese intermediate goods, the world will suffer from the consequences of oversupply and agonize over protectionism. But Korea may have to bear the brunt of the typhoon. The United States and Europe can set up protective barriers against a barrage of cheap Chinese goods, but Korea can't. The problem may loom larger than the risks posed by Project Finance crisis. This is the reason why we must keep a sharp eye on China's continued commitment to overproduction and aggressive export strategy.

PART 2
Change of International Politics

Global Economy under Geopolitical Change

US-China Competition for Greater Power Becomes Systemic[1]

1. China as a Mediator in the Middle East?

Archrivals Saudi Arabia and Iran agreed to restore diplomatic relations, a breakthrough brokered by Beijing on March 10th, a news as stunning as the "Nixon Shock" in July 1971 when U.S. President Richard Nixon announced that he would visit China. Nixon and his point man for foreign affairs Kissinger helped the communist China's long overdue reform and opening up with a view to isolating the Soviet economy. As is widely known, this has led to the dismantlement of the Soviet Union. China-brokered rapprochement between pro-American Saudi Arabia and anti-American Iran is heralding a great upheaval not only in the region but also throughout the world.

Now being energy-independent on foreign energy with its surging production of shale oil, the U.S. is taking a hands-

---

[1] This column was published on March 20, 2023.

off approach toward the Middle East. In order to fill the power vacuum and to guarantee the security of regional allies, Washington envisioned an alliance of collective security similar to NATO in the Middle East, and against this background came signing of the Abraham Accords in September 2020. As NATO is a defensive alliance of European countries against Russia, the Abraham Accords refers to the Middle East defense alliance against Iranian threats. Israel and the UAE reached a historic peace deal to normalize diplomatic relations, and Morocco, Egypt, and Sudan joined other Arab nations agreeing to establish full diplomatic relations with Israel. Saudi Arabia, as well, says they are ready for joining the accords. The weird and unlikely Mideast alliance between the Sunni Muslim countries and the Jewish state to form an "anti-Iran" front has finally come into being.

However, the China-brokered new agreement between Iran and Saudi Arabia to restore diplomacy has made a major crack on the epic Abraham Accords, making it difficult for the accords to proceed. The Sunni and Shiite split in the Islamic world is comparable to that of the Roman Catholic and Eastern Orthodox in the medieval Christianity. They don't see each other as being Muslims and their relations have been increasingly marked by deadly conflicts. Surprisingly, the archrivals were brought together by Communist China, making one of its greatest diplomatic feats. Does this mean, as many people view, China has taken the mantle of responsibility and the role of a direct mediator in the complicated geopolitics of the Middle East armed with its economic power as the world's largest oil importer?

As national security is definitely the most compelling government interest, nations can sacrifice economy for security, but not vice versa. Economy is about profit, and security is about survival, so they are in two completely different dimensions. Therefore, it is absurd to say that China's economic power made the deal between Saudi Arabia and Iran possible. Then, what was the secret behind China's successful mediation in the geopolitical structure of the Middle East? Saudi Arabia and Iran have long been rivals, but they do have something in common to be concerned about.

2. Outdated Debates on State Governance System

1) Beginning of competition for State Governance System

Debates on state governance systems are the outcome of the Cold War (1945-1991). Contrary to Karl Marx's prediction of socialism's triumph over capitalism in his theory of scientific socialism, the Great Depression did not bring down capitalistic countries. Rather, the communist revolution took place in Russia and China, two of the least developed countries, and their urbanization and industrialization took place only after the introduction of socialist systems.

After the Russian Revolution of 1917, Stalin collectivized farms, which was largely viewed as a disastrous decision. The Soviets skipped expanding capital base of light industries and jumped straight into fostering heavy industries. In about 20 years later, the Soviet Union was able to emerge as a leading industrial country in the world. It was the only European country that could fight against Germany, the most advanced country during World War II and indeed the Soviets did the vast majority of fighting and won the war. The world's political and economic elites and intellectuals marveled at the Soviet Union and began to seriously consider introducing a Soviet-style system in their countries.

The aftermath of World War II was the beginning of a new era defined by the fall of all colonial empires which was precipitated by the United States. American-style liberal democracy and market economy were introduced to newly created nations. Some latecomers, however, were more attracted to the Soviet development models. As they were in their fragile state, liberal democracy meant social chaos and laissez-faire market economy was synonymous with incompetent government.

Some of latecomer countries were strongly enticed to the Soviet development model. It seemed less liberal but safe from political and social chaos, and the centralized planned economy was believed to speed up development by mobilizing all the resources of the country. The public were attracted to communist 'equality', and the elite expected that the Soviet model would enable rapid 'development'. Many new countries, voluntarily or unwillingly, had to make a choice between liberal democracy plus market economy and socialism with planned economic system. That was the start of full-fledged battle of ideas.

2) Command Economy on the Offensive

Production and consumption in a market economy are largely driven by price. As the price increases, production rises while consumption declines and as the price falls, supply declines while demand rises. Mainstream economists used to criticize the socialist planned economy saying 'if the price mechanism is removed, who would decide when and what to produce and how much? That is simply impossible!' This a.k.a. "socialist calculation debate" revolved around the question that even if central planners can, in principle at least, make the economic calculation regarding production and distribution of hundred-thousands of goods and services for millions of people, this certainly would result in tremendous inefficient allocation of society's economic resources.

Different from what was expected, however, the Soviet Union, a command economy, survived World War II and even further, continued to record post-war economic growth and people began to rethink. Wassily Leontief (1905-1999), an American economist of Russian decent invented input-output tables in 1936, and when computers were able to calculate hundreds of thousands of matrix tables, the tedious and annoying 'calculation' became realistic. A computer in its early days of development, was just a computing or calculating device.

In the 1960s, under the banner of 'modified capitalism', free market economies as well began to make economic growth plans and mobilize national resources with advancement in mathematics and statistics as well. Now, both socialism and capitalism use government intervention and regulation of business, except that they differ in the scope. Simply put, the "calculation debate" has become pointless.

Instead, the Soviet system seemed to have proved itself more advanced in the field of science and technology. The MiG-15, the first Soviet jet, unveiled in 1947, outperformed American fighter jects. The Soviet Union was abreast with the U.S. in the nuclear arms race, and it also launched the earth's first artificial satellite (the Shock of Sputnik in 1957). The Soviets developed the MiG-15 based on jet engine technology given by the naive British Labor Party government as a gesture of goodwill with reservation not to be used for military purposes. And the Soviet development of nuclear weapons was a feat of effective intelligence gathering. The launch of the satellite was also a work of German scientists kidnapped from Berlin. It was outcome of national projects supported by mobilizing all the resources of the country. But at any rate it was the Soviet Union that appeared to be winning in in the race with the U.S. in the fields of science and technology.

The 1970s oil crisis sent shockwaves throughout Western economies, but the Soviet economy, an oil exporting country, enjoyed a great boom and grew to 70% of the size of the U.S. economy. It seemed only a matter of time before the Soviet Union caught up with the U.S. And Harvard University professor Paul Samuelson, then a rising star economist in the U.S. put out a gloomy outlook that Soviet GNP would exceed that of the United States by the mid-1980s. The prospect that Russia, one of the least developed countries in Europe at the beginning of the 20th century, might overtake the United States, the world's most powerful country, was a shock to the political and economic elites of the time. Against this backdrop, the socialism craze swept across the world in the 1970s.

3) Pricing Mechanisms and Knowledge Issues

The Soviet system began to show its weakness in the mid-1980s in the fields of light industry and consumer goods.

Soviet citizens suffered from chronic shortage of consumer goods due the Soviet economy's prioritizing military technology and heavy industry. The Soviets bartered oil and gas for consumer goods from other European countries. But as the imported commodities decreased with the decline of the oil prices, Soviet citizens found increasingly empty shelves in the supermarkets in Moscow. The Soviet economy failed to provide quality pencils and notebooks for children, and Gorbachev who was appointed General Secretary in 1985 lamented "Imagine a country that launches satellites and it can't resolve the problem of women's pantyhose."

The price mechanism is not simply the forces of demand and supply. Friedrich Hayek pointed out in his 1988 book, *The Fatal Conceit* that the price system is a mechanism for gathering and utilizing dispersed information across a society efficiently.

Let's say, a $1 pencil is supplied in a perfectly competitive market. One day person A came across an idea in a book and was able to produce the pencil at the price of 90 cents. Now A gained excess profit, and consumers could save 10 cents. 'Hidden or Unearthed knowledge' was used in the production process.

Then, a jealous competitor B worked on for many days and nights and came up with a new method to produce the pencils for 80 cents. Now, B replacing A enjoys the excess profit, and the consumer saves 20 cents. This time 'created knowledge' was used in the production process.

In a market economy, prices serve as signals to see whether resources and knowledge of a society are allocated efficiently. A realized a $1 pencil isn't efficient and introduced a 90-cent production process. Then, competitor B who sees his business slow down, devises an innovative production process cutting the price to 80 cents. In the process, 'hidden knowledge' and 'created knowledge' are generated for the good of the society. No one determines nor intervenes when, where, and how much is produced. Prices send signals to allocate all the resources and knowledge of the society in the most efficient ways. This is the source of wealth and prosperity of market economies.

The Soviet system, unable to provide citizens with basic necessities of life, collapsed in 1991. The contest of two ideologies has ended, and liberal democracy and market economy have emerged as the modern state system. The Soviet Union and the Eastern Bloc recognized their problems and moved quickly to implement systemic transition. However, in the process of the big-bang approach to transition, their economy fell into chaos and communist parties in the countries lost power.

3. Second Round of Systemic Competition

1) Muslim States in Defiance

The Islamic world, though, had different ideas. They agreed that liberal democracy and market economy are better for their national development, but devout Muslims hated the social changes that capitalism would bring. Their frugal and simple life, they worried, would turn into life of luxury and extravagance. Families would fall apart, divorce rates would rise, and there would be more abandoned children. Obscene music and videos would be played under the pretext of "freedom of expression." They feared that democratic capitalism would undermine their religion, traditions, customs, and culture, leading to promiscuity and vulgarity.

Despite the many advantages of liberal democracy and market economy that had ascended to a universal value, dismantling traditional culture to be brought about by them was completely unacceptable in the pious Islamic world. Moreover, it was the system that was built by Christianity, the enemy of Islam.

Sayyid Qutb (1906-1966), a leading Muslim Brotherhood ideologue was one of the most prominent and influential critics of Western civilization. He was a university graduate and one of a few Muslim intellectuals who understood Western civilization, At the age of 42 Qutb went to the United States on a government scholarship to study the Western system, but instead grew strongly disapproving of American culture and society that were after money and pleasure.

On his return to Egypt, Qutb published "The America that I Have Seen", where he became explicitly critical of American society, being prosperous but one of the most corrupt civilizations. In later years he wrote a manifesto of political Islam called *Milestones*, upholding his radical Islamic fundamentalism based on his interpretations of the Qur'an. Qutb and his Islamic fundamentalism were a threat even to hardline Arab nationalist president Gamal Abdel Nasser who put him in jail and sentenced to death.

Sayyid Qutb was a martyr in the eyes of his followers and his teachings influenced on the rise of Islamic fundamentalism. The Islamic resurgence has led to the 1979 Iranian Revolution, the Taliban's takeover of Afghanistan, the 9/11 attacks by Al Qaeda in 2001, and the ISIS movement to reestablish the caliphate. They rejected modernity and capitalistic development not because they did not know how, but because they knew too well what would come with it.

2) What Saudi Arabia and Iran Have in Common

Here lies Saudi Arabia's major concern. The modern Kingdom of Saudi Arabia was founded in 1932 by Ibn Saud and its legitimacy hinges upon its acknowledged status as custodians of the Holy Sites of Islam in Mecca and Medina. Oil revenues have helped Saudi rulers to buy the support of its citizens. The Saudis have been enjoying one of the most lavish welfare systems in the world thanks to royal family's oil industry, so they shut their eyes to minor violations of freedom and human rights.

However, with Europe and the US moving towards renewable energy, the future of oil and gas is not very bright. Stagnant oil demand and falling prices would push Saudi Arabia's economy to the corner and the Saudi royal family could no longer neglect a fresh wave of industrialization which they have kept at bay to stay in power. Crown Prince Mohammed bin Salman, already de facto ruler, has unveiled his big plans to modernize the kingdom.

However, the absolute monarchy ruled by the Saud dynasty may be brought to an end if civil uprisings demanding for more freedom and human rights break out during the process of the modernization. Or its Western-style modernization may face strong opposition from the Wahhabi religious establishment, another pillar of the regime, eventually undermining the dynasty's legitimacy. Saudi Arabia faces a conundrum of pushing for industrialization while at the same time preserving the monarchy and the Islamic way of life.

The same goes for United Republicans of Iran. For 45 years after the 1979 the Islamic Revolution, religious leaders' promises of heavenly state have not been fulfilled, and Iran is reeling from the long-standing isolation from the international community due to its anti-Americanism. Its economy, once in competition for supremacy with the

Saudis in the region, has shrunk in its size to less than half of Saudi Arabia's. Reforms are necessary for Iran to end the isolation and the first step for that end is to bury the hatchet with its neighboring countries.

Pursuing reforms, however, are like admitting the failure of the Islamic Revolution, and ending hostile relations with Sunni Arab countries may shake the Shia theocracy at the root. In October 2022, Iranian women, in their fight for human rights, took to the streets to protest mandatory hijab. Religious police cracked down the protest by force, but a further deterioration of the situation might lead to a color revolution, eventually overthrowing the Iranian government.

Saudi Arabia and Iran, both on their way to reforms, also need a stronger governing system to tackle social disorder that could arise in the process of social restructuring. Western systems won't do, but Chinese model can be the answer.

3) Chinese State Governance System and Its Implications

In his 1989 essay, *The End of History?* Francis Fukuyama

predicted there will be no longer any ideological competitor for liberal democracy and market economy in the future, and the collapse of the Soviet Union in 1991 seemed to be a testament to it. As Eastern Bloc countries, as well as East Asian socialist countries such as China and Vietnam rushed to convert to free economies, debates over the state systems became seemingly meaningless. In the modern state system, the market economy and liberal democracy are like the two wheels of a cart, so it was understood that China's transition to a market economy meant that it would sooner or later be a liberal democracy.

But China was different. The Soviet Union and Eastern Europe took a 'big-bang' approach to economic and political changes in which they introduced a market economy and political democratization like multi-party system and direct elections all together and went downhill 30 years ago, but Chinese socialism has not only survived for over 45 years after its opening-up in 1978, but also continues to evolve and develop in the 21st century.

China's economy has employed the market economy model that recognizes individual freedom of occupation and private property rights, although the huge state-owned enterprises are under direct control of Communist

Party. But on the political front, China is a one-party state and the ruling Communist party influences and oversees almost every aspect of life from politics, economy, society, to culture (in Chinese terms, it is called the collective leadership of the Communist Party of China). This is typical of the Communist Party of the former Soviet Union.

However, the citizens of the free world, having seen the disastrous failure of the Mao Zedong's Great Leap Forward and the Cultural Revolution, do not know how the communist party has changed since Deng Xiaoping's economic reforms. In order to implement reforms and opening-up, revolutionary cadres with little education have been replaced with bureaucratic technocrats and the command economy has transitioned to a mixed economy where local governments and enterprises can make economic decisions as long as they do not go against the central government's policies. China has also implemented an explicit ban on one-man domination and personality cults, embracing the notion of collective leadership, and has publicly emphasized on governing the country in accordance with Chinese constitution and laws.

The hard control mechanisms by judicial and armed forces are still prominent in China, but the soft control mechanisms of controlling organizations and media to persuade the public are also actively working. Uyghur concentration camps in Xinjiang, controversial Hong Kong security law, and anti-government protests during the COVID-19 pandemic got the international attention, but only a few out of 1.4 billion Chinese people came directly under severe oppression.

China's social credit system, facial recognition technology, and media censorship including the Internet and social media are also problematic, but a majority of the Chinese public view them inevitable to prevent rebellious elements that may harm social stability that they had achieved after 45 years of arduous reforms and opening up. The approval rating of the Chinese central government has been hovering around 80-90% since the 2000s.

The Communist Party of China has more than 95 million members who have passed a rigorous selection process, drawing strong support from the people. Only 8% of the members are party and government cadres, equivalent to civil servants, and the rest are civilians, working as passionate supporters of the current system. Demands for democratization have long been silenced after the

Tiananmen Square massacre and instead, in the prevailing patriotism young elite college students aspire to become a Party member. How is this possible?

This may give the solution to the problems faced by Saudi Arabia and Iran. They must be able to aptly respond to the people's growing demand for freedom and democracy on their way to reform. It is not something to be addressed by simply introducing Chinese control systems on social media and facial recognition technology. They need a comprehensive study and analysis of China's state governing system and its knowhows accumulated for more than 45-years of experience. To adopt the unrevealed and incomprehensible Chinese governing system, the two countries need to turn to China.

4. Systemic Competition Gearing Up

China's mediation in the complex geopolitical structure of the Middle East was possible because Saudi Arabia and Iran have security interests to obtain from China. It is not a matter of exterior security but of interior security. That is, the Chinese state governance system.

In fact, a majority of countries around the world do not place a priority on liberal democracy as much as the Western societies. A nation's foremost responsibility is to bring security and prosperity to its people and China is, undeniably, one of the countries that has accomplished that goal in the shortest period of time.

The universal values that the Western system upholds is still great, but only two countries, Korea and Taiwan have succeeded in market economy under liberal democracy for more than 70 years after the end of World War II. Singapore has been the classic illustration of soft authoritarianism where the People's Action Party has been one of the longest-ruling parties in the world. It has been 30 years since Fukuyama declared 'the end of history', but only about 20% of the world's population enjoys freedom and democracy in prosperity, and the rest of the world is still under dictatorships or, at best, people are left unattended in incomplete freedom, or freedom to be out of work or starvation.

What would happen if the elites of these countries introduced a Chinese-style state governance system in hopes of developing their nation? Middle East countries and Central Asia that are rich in resources are already on the way, and underdeveloped countries in Latin America and Africa are turning to Beijing expecting China's economic support. UAE's recent purchase of Chinese fighter jets and Vietnam's Communist Party leadership occupied by pro-China figures are demonstrative of a profound shift to authoritarianism.

China is no longer a Soviet-style command economy. It has a system in which the price mechanism is working and therefore knowledge is transferred and made the most of in pursuit of individual's ends as Hayek pointed out. China has succeeded to some extent in catching up with developed countries with an input driven growth model and a catch-up strategy, but it remains to be seen whether it can make creation and innovation under the leadership of the Communist Party. Now, the second-round of competition for a state governance system is gearing up.

Rivalry between the U.S. and China goes beyond a mere conflict of national interests and extends to systemic confrontation between American-style liberal democracy and socialism with Chinese characteristics. It is an ominous reminder of the Cold War between the U.S. and Soviet Union. If China tries to spread "socialism with Chinese characteristics" as the Soviet Union did to expand socialist system how will the world order change in the years to come?

Will the U.S. compromise by restricting China's access to high-tech industries and finance but in the meantime allowing its trade in low- and medium-value products? Or will it go extreme by taking a full-scale containment strategy like it did against the Soviet Union? Korea that has deep economic times with both the U.S. and China. It is imperative that it needs to pay close attention to the hegemony competition between the United States and China as it evolves into systemic confrontation.

References

1. 『Chinese Governance System I, II』, Yeong-nam Cho, 21st Century Books
   Reference is made from the chapters explaining Chinese governance system. The book offers a pertinent analysis from an empirical rather than an ideological perspective and provides a better understanding of recent changes in the Chinese governance system.

Shifting U.S. Middle East Policy[1]

1. Origin and Essence of Conflict in the Middle East

Amid Russia's ongoing war on Ukraine an armed conflict between Israel and Hamas has been taking place in and around the Gaza Strip since October 2023. As the Israeli military stepped up its operation in Gaza resulting in massive casualties, the Houthi rebels, in response, attacked Western cargo ships transiting in the Red Sea. The United States has launched airstrikes and is assembling a multinational naval coalition to help safeguard commercial traffic in the Red Sea. Are war clouds hovering over the Middle East again, the powder keg of the world?

The Ottoman Empire's westward expansion after overthrowing Constantinople in 1453 has posed an existential threat to Europe. But the Sykes-Picot Agreement between Britain and France in 1916 ended the threat once and for all. The size of the Ottoman Empire was reduced to the capital Istanbul and Anatolia peninsula. Britain

---

[1] This column was published on March 18, 2024.

and France divided up the Arab territories of the former Ottoman Empire, drawing borders by the latitude and the longitude and creating monarchies in collusion with the tribal chiefs in the region.

No one knew that the Levant area[2] and the 'man-made' states in the Arabian Peninsula, which were carved up to check Russia's southward advance and stabilize trade routes to India, would seed deep-rooted rancor between Islamic and Christian civilizations. The largely desert areas of the Middle East, historically known for fishing and transit ports turned out to be a treasure trove of petroleum during the interwar periods of World Wars I and II.

The irrelevant borders that crisscrossed deserts and wastelands in the Middle East has now been entangled in conflicts of interest over the oil fields. It is true that things have become by far more complicated after the modern country of Israel was formed in the Middle East. However, it is only a biased argument to say that there will be peace in the Middle East if Israel is not there. Greedy monarchs in the region claimed that the land - more frankly speaking,

---

[2] The Levant derives its name from Italian levante, "rising", hinting at the direction the Sun rises. It refers to Lebanon, Syria, Israel, and Jordan on the Eastern Mediterranean coast.

the oil reserves in it - was theirs, citing historical, religious, tribal, racial, or whatever reasons they could think of.

The United States commitment to rebuild Europe after the World War II made it necessary to resolve the Middle East issue. It makes sense that the oil out of the soil on the "New World" or the American continents is consumed in the same region and likewise, the oil found in the "Old World" is used in Europe. Europe has large volume of oil and gas reserves in Russia and Romania. But that was not a viable option when the US adopted a containment policy to restrict Soviet's global power. In order to give Europe an access to Middle East oil, the US had to stabilize the region. So, it helped Iran and Saudi Arabia ward off the threat from the Soviet inroads in the Middle East and ensured the safe passage of ships in the Straits of Hormuz and Suez Canal.

Complicated history and vast oil reserves has made the Middle East a hot spot in international geopolitics since the end of the World War II. U.S. crude oil production hit a peak of 9 million barrels a day, allowing it to be energy independent. But as the production declined to 4 million barrels in the 1970s the stability in the Middle East has become a vital issue for the United States as well. The 1979 revolution transformed Iran from a pillar of the U.S. Middle East policy into a threat to the regional status quo, so the strategic partnership with the Kingdom of Saudi Arabia has become more important. The United States stationed troops - Navy, Air Force and Army - in the Middle East to safeguard the European economy or its own economy. The U.S. Armed Forces completed their withdrawal from Afghanistan in 2021, marking the end of land force pull-out from the Middle East.

Ever since its involvement in the Middle East affairs, Washington had to make a great number of strategic decisions and made quite a few mistakes in the process. One of them is the U.S.- and British-instigated royal coup in 1953 that toppled the elected Prime Minister of Iran, Mohammad Mossadegh, causing Iran to turn anti-American. Another mistake was made during the 1980-89 Iran-Iraq War. Washington aided Saddam Hussein to prevent Iran's victory, but ended up contributing to militarizing Iraq. In 2003, the United States launched a major military invasion of Iraq. However, the fall of Saddam Hussein led to the worst outcome, the rise of ISIS and other militant groups. The U.S. also betrayed the Kurds, who was a military partner in the fight against ISIS. And in 2021 U.S. left behind hundreds of thousands of Afghan collaborators in chaotic withdrawal from the war in Afghanistan that lasted two decades since 2001.

After the World War II, the United States was viewed as a liberator who brought independence and liberal democracy to those under colonial rules. But to Middle Easterners, the United States is nothing but a neo-imperialist or Machiavellian manipulator. If it were not for oil, the United States would like to walk away from the Middle East politics and end their decades-long hostility. The time has finally come.

2. Budget Constrains of the U.S. Government

The present U.S. economic expansion is comparable to the 1960s' prosperity. It thrives in global competitiveness across all industries - not to mention the primary sector including agriculture, and the entire tertiary sector such as education, finance, media, entertainment, engineering services, exemplified by big tech companies. In the secondary sector, manufacturing has recently been in decline. But the emergence of Apple and Tesla and their high value-added products brought about the huge international sales in the automobile and consumer electronics industries, contributing to restoring U.S. industrial leadership.

The U.S. energy crisis of the 1970s is no longer a problem. As of 2023, the United States produced 13.6 million barrels a day and imported 3.3 million barrels from Canada and 1 million barrels from Mexico, achieving energy self-sufficiency in North America. Venture companies that mushroomed during the shale boom have undergone mergers and acquisitions by big oil companies such as ExxonMobil, Chevron, and Occidental. As long as the U.S. can produce enough oil for its use using the country's oil refining and cracking facilities, there is no need to import oil anymore. Then its oil interests in the Middle East will disappear within a few years.

Economists often cite the twin deficits in the trade and finances as major concerns for the U.S. economy. As a matter of fact, the trade deficit is not a threat at all. The trade deficit of about $800 billion to $1 trillion dollars comes down to $200 billion dollars in the current account balance where the services balance, interest, and dividends are included. Additionally, the U.S. capital account surplus and huge financial assets up to $70 trillion overshadow the meager trade deficit of $1 trillion.

The trade deficit, in fact, is a problem for countries like Korea, which import raw materials and capital goods in exchange for dollars. The United States doesn't have to care about trade balance because it has the issuing power of the dollar, the primary reserve currency for international transactions. The U.S. trade deficit simply indicates an income inequality problem that hollowing out of the country's manufacturing sector takes away jobs from the middle class, mainly from the people without a college degree. In that sense, it is just a domestic political problem.

Fiscal deficit is a serious problem, though. The United States' national debt has exceeded 120% of GDP. And its budget deficit once reached 15% of GDP in just one year during the Covid-19 lockdowns, still lingering around 6.3% in 2023. These numbers are well over the 3% ceiling for the budget deficit maintained by EU governments, showing the United States is in no position to criticize budget deficit in Southern European countries. S&P and Fitch downgraded the U.S. credit rating to AA+. Moody's maintained it at the highest Aaa level, but lowered the U.S. credit ratings outlook from stable to negative.

The best way to reduce the fiscal deficit is to cut spending. But in a country where congressional elections take place every two years, reducing welfare benefits is a very difficult decision. Cutting defense spending instead, which amounts to $886 billion per year (3% of GDP, 12% of the government budget) could be one of the easiest solutions. For now, that is far from easy because the United States needs to increase its military budget to counter China, just as the Reagan administration did to contain the Soviet Union in the 1980s.

Against this backdrop, the next step is to call for defense spending in Western Europe and East Asia that have become rich in the international security order cultivated and maintained by the United States. If NATO members increase their defense spending only 1% of GDP, the military budget will amount to $200 billion. And Washington is likely to demand for burden-sharing among their allies in the Asia-Pacific region as well.

The choices left for the U.S. are clear now - either reduce defense spending and use it to pay debt, or focus its military spending on the arms race with China. If unrest breaks out in the Middle East, the United States is no longer able to intervene as it did in the past. Europe must pick up the baton.

3. New Middle East Police: NATO

Historically, it was not the United States but Europe that has had interest in the Middle East. It is evident in the history like the Persian Wars and Eastern Expedition of Alexander the Great. And that was the reason why the Eastern Roman Empire had its capital in Constantinople. The Crusades and the Siege of Constantinople were, in essence, religious conflicts between Christianity and Islam. The U.S. intervention has been necessary in the Middle East affairs to give assistance to Western Europe in ruins after the war since 1945, but now Europe is responsible for the challenges coming from the Middle East.

At the moment, military conflicts are largely confined to Gaza and the Red Sea, but problems may arise anywhere and at any time in the Middle East. For instance, the deadly bombings at the fourth anniversary of the death of Qasem Soleimani, a former commander of the IRGC in January this year were carried out by the Islamic State (ISIS), which was reported to have been rooted out. Arab monarchies such as the UAE, Qatar, and Kuwait are wealthy but weak. And their neighboring republics such as Iran, Iraq, and Syria are poor and violent. It is like luxury mansions standing at the end of a messy, violent street full of the impoverished.

The Biden administration brokered the Abraham Accords, a series of agreements on Arab-Israeli normalization in a bid to form an anti-Iran alliance led by Israel and Saudi Arabia. It was a typical policy for regional power balance, but it is unclear whether it is viable. If disruption occurs in the Middle East, will America intervene as in the past? Instead, Europe will have to send NATO forces. For it has no other option but to get oil from the Middle East, with Russian oil no longer available.

Former U.S. president Donald Trump questions whether NATO still has a purpose, now that the Soviet Union is gone and replaced by a weak Russia. Someday Korea may be asked to make a contribution to maintaining security in the Strait of Hormuz and the Red Sea. Are we ready to deal with it, if requested to join the NATO+ (NATO Plus) maritime security operations?

Now, the ROK-US alliance alone will not guarantee our future. During the old Cold War, Korea was protected by the Western powers for geopolitical reasons, but in the new Cold War, Korea will no doubt be asked to make a contribution to the West. More specifically, about what role Korea will play when the NATO undertakes a new peacekeeping mission in the Middle East.

Lord Palmerston of England said, "We have no eternal allies, and we have no perpetual enemies. Our interests are eternal and perpetual, and those interests it is our duty to follow." But this is just the words of the Britain's former prime minister in the era of Pax Britannica. As the world we live in today becomes more and more like a jungle, any misstep would be irrecoverable for smaller countries.

Netanyahu Ignites the Powder Keg Waiting to Blow[1)]

The armed conflict between Israel and Hamas, a Palestinian militant group in the Gaza Strip, has continued over a year since 7 October 2023 and now is spreading throughout the Middle East. The 'two-state solution', proposed as part of Oslo Accords[2)] was unacceptable from the outset to Hamas and the Likud Party led by Israeli Prime Minister Benjamin Netanyahu. Fierce counterattack by Israel in response to Hamas' terror attack has left the Gaza Strip devastated and the death toll reached 40,000, which prompted anti-Israel protests across Europe and the United States.

Since its foundation in 1948, Israel has been viewed in the Western hemisphere as a victim and a minority significantly outnumbered in the Middle East, which gives

---

1) This column was published on October 10, 2024.
2) The 1993 Oslo Accords brokered by US President Bill Clinton are a set of agreements in which Israel and the Palestine Liberation Organization has accepted the concept of a "two state solution," or peaceful coexistence.

it a right to use force in self-defense. However, the Gaza war has been a diplomatic disaster for Israel, destroying its reputation capital that it has built up in the West over the past 70 years and turning it into an international pariah.

Israel is no longer considered a victim in Palestine violence, but a perpetrator who persecutes Palestinian people, and Jews are accused of committing genocide in Gaza, comparable to the Holocaust they had suffered under the Nazi regime. In the end, there is a growing suspicion that Israel's ultimate goal is not a free democratic state where Jews and Palestinians coexist, but rather a Jewish national state in Palestine, or a Zionist state.

There is a large Muslim population in Europe and the United States. In particular, Europe has seen a massive migration of Muslims since Color Revolutions in the Middle East and North Africa and their political leverage in Europe is growing stronger as well. Now that the anti-Israel narrative was growing louder among progressive intellectuals, journalists, universities, and social groups, many political leaders including the Democratic Party of the United States joined criticizing Israel. Jewish elites around the world and Israelis were stunned to see the anti-Jewish protests taking place all over the world.

However, Netanyahu government silenced the anti-Semitic movements at a single stroke, taking a bold move to launch an all-out war against Hezbollah in Lebanon and the Houthis in Yemen. It is well known that Hamas, Hezbollah, and the Houthis have worked as proxies of Iran, a regional troublemaker, but these violent non-state actors were tinderboxes, too dangerous to touch. Strictly speaking, Hamas is an internal affair of Israel, and so is Hezbollah to Lebanon, or in dispute with Israel on a larger scale. Yemen is a barren soil that the international community would hardly give a second look at if safe passage through the Red Sea was guaranteed.

However, the West was aware that a great number of Christians had been expelled or killed in Lebanon since the 1970s, and that the Houthis were escalating cross-border attacks, striking oil facilities in Saudi Arabia and the UAE. The Houthi rebels have carried out hundreds of attacks on Western merchant ships crossing the Red Sea since the war in Gaza.

The West has turned a deaf ear to the pleas of displaced Christians who fled Lebanon from Hezbollah's persecution and has brushed aside the Yemeni conflict as a regional issue. There is little argument that the Red Sea crisis must be addressed, but Western container shipping lines are advised to choose the lengthier route via the Cape of Good Hope avoiding the Red Sea. As a result, the revenue of Egypt's Suez Canal has declined by almost 30%.

The Middle East with its knotty religious, ethnic, cultural and linguistic diversity faces three major threats: the Arab-Israeli rivalry, the Sunni-Shia discord and the tension between the monarchies and the Islamic Republic. In substance, the Israeli-Palestinian conflict is nothing more than a regional issue, and the Sunni-Shia discord is more or less ideological, similar to the black-white racial conflict in the United States or the Korea-Japan disputes in East Asia, both of which are rooted in history. In contrast, the conflict between the monarchies and the Islamic Republic is a clash for the national system, and an existential threat to the rulers of the monarchy. Moreover, it is a 3,000-year-old face-off between Arabs and Persians.

Hamas, Hezbollah, and the Houthis are anti-monarchy as well as anti-Israel. They share the same goal of destroying the state of Israel, but their final goal is to overthrow the monarchy and build an Islamic republic in the Middle East with Iran. In that case, Iran would be able to exercise control over the oil fields on both sides of the Persian

Gulf, as the leader of the Islamic republic countries. It means that Iran will have the dominant power over the global energy market. It would be a great feat for Teheran showing the world the legitimacy of the 1979 Iranian Revolution that toppled the monarchy and established the Islamic Republic. More importantly, it would be a boon to the Iranian people who have been suffering under economic sanctions from the United States.

As Israel launched a wave of huge airstrikes targeting Hezbollah and the Houthis following its offensive against Hamas, the monarchies of the Middle East, not to mention the Western countries which have been sitting on the fence, were taken by surprise. Criticism of Israel's actions has dissipated, and instead Israel is acclaimed for its adroitness and audacity in carrying out what the West has not dared to do fearing political ramifications and substantial risks that might follow.

The monarchies of the Middle East are also at a crucial crossroads. While Israel is waging war against Iran's proxies threatening the monarchy and when an all-out war with Iran appears imminent, which side should Midde East monarchies take in an Iran-Israel war? For them, the Islamic Republic is an unacceptable option and accordingly

Iran is a grave threat to the system.

Saudi Arabia recalibrated its foreign policy strengthening ties with Russia and China in the event of the U.S. withdrawal from the Middle East, while the UAE signed a strategic partnership with France. Sitting on one of the world's largest gas and oil reserves, the UAE has made a landmark deal with South Korea to build nuclear power plants, saying it was preparing for life after oil run-out. However, it is obvious that it was a part of its ambition to be a nuclear power. For Arab monarchies with smaller populations and weak political support despite their wealth, the threat from Iran is real and viable. And the threat has reached their doorstep through a network of Iran's proxies.

Israel is capable of defending itself and does not need to step between Arabs and Iran. But Hamas and Hezbollah have become an existential threat to Israel. If Israel directly hits Iran going beyond Iran's proxies, all of its efforts to coexist with Arabs would come to nothing and Israel would find itself become a prime target for all terrorist groups in the Middle East. That is why the Western allies and Middle Eastern monarchies have been reluctant to stir the hornets' nest.

However, a liberal democratic country cannot go without elections. If Prime Minister Netanyahu fails to win the election, he would face the end of his political career and even end up in jail. Netanyahu, dubbed as a cat with nine lives as he is the longest-serving prime minister, is trying to save himself by pushing for a war with Iran, which could bring Israel down into an abyss of endless war and terrorism. As was well demonstrated by Xi Jinping and the princelings in China and Kim Jong-un in North Korea, political leadership are more inclined to exercise their political power in their private interests, rather than in the public one.

Presumably, Netanyahu views that coexistence of the monarchies and Iran is unfeasible and that a war is just a matter of time. He may think he has only sparked a fire a little earlier. Korea relies on the Middle East for 90% of its energy supply and must watch closely as the tensions between Israel and Iran are growing worryingly close to boiling over, which would inevitably bring destructive aftershocks in the global energy market.

The Potential Impact of Trump's Return[1]

1. Bracing for Trump's Return

It certainly looked like that the upcoming U.S. presidential election was going to be a bitterly contested rematch of the former president Donald Trump vs. Joe Biden the incumbent, which were viewed to be unpredictable to the last minute. However, the failed assassination attempt on Trump on July 14 gave him a boost for his chance for another term. Republican presidential candidate Trump, wounded and bleeding, raised his fist in defiance on the podium, clearly showing who the strong man was. Many voters have chosen bravery over smartness when casting ballots for political leaders. The Democratic Party fell under mounting pressure to dump the Biden card and come up with a new, young and capable candidate.

What would Donald Trump's second term look like? Trump has been outspoken about rolling back key policies

---

[1] This column was published on July 22, 2024.

that Biden put in place and running an aggressive second term upon his return to the White House. However, even so he has only 4 years to serve together with the Senate under Democrats' control, in the highly decentralized U.S. political decision-making system.

During the presidential campaign in 2019, Biden slammed then President Trump's tariffs on China but after taking office, he expanded Trump's anti-China policy, in fact taking a more aggressive stance. If Trump wins the 2024 election, he may also take some of Biden's policies over and put his own spin on them. However, for the most part, Trump's second administration is expected to be wildly different from the former government, which will be looked over in the following.

2. Ending the Ukraine War

First of all, Donald Trump has repeatedly said he could settle the war between Russia and Ukraine in one day if he's elected president again. The Russian invasion of Ukraine is a major event that has brought about the collapse of the German economic business model.

For decades, Germany's economic prosperity was mainly based on the imports of cheap energy and resources from Russia in return for industrial and technological exports. In the meantime, German manufacturers have kept their competitive edge backed by cheap energy. Germany, as a status quo power, has made the most out of the EU, the world's second largest market. At the same time, it exports products and industrial technology to China with a view to gaining access to the vast Chinese market. In all, this forms an economic triangle of Germany, Russia, and China.

However, this collides with America's global policy. The United States, being the sole hegemon since the end of Cold War, has seldom interfered with intercontinental and international trade relationships. However, the inexplicit goal of the U.S. foreign policy is 'to keep the Old World countries from accessing to the New World and to prevent the emergence of regional hegemons in the Old World.' To that end, maintaining the regional balance of power is the key.

The Old World consists of Europe and Asia. Germany and Russia are widely seen as potential hegemons in Europe, and so are China and Japan in Asia. In this geopolitical context, Germany might have come to catapult Russia and China to two regional hegemons in the Old World unwittingly, by having close economic ties with the two countries.

Undoubtedly, Kremlin's invasion of Ukraine puts an end to the German-Russian economic alliance. Germany's export of industrial technology to Russia in return for cheap energy, will eventually strengthen Russia, making Germany's eastern border dangerous. The 50 year-long energy alliance between Germany and Russia, which started with the arrival of the first Soviet gas deliveries in 1973, is now over. Thus the German manufacturing industry based on cheap Russian oil is declining at a fast pace.

A ceasefire in Ukraine may open the door for Russia to return to the international energy and financial markets, but its chances of obtaining industrial technology that it needs for its success are slim to none. There are only five countries in the world that have both technologies and production capabilities in manufacturing sector: the United States, Japan, Germany, Korea, and China. Excluding the United States, Japan and Germany, Russia has only South Korea and China to turn to. And this is why Vladimir Putin keeps waving an olive branch at South Korea while forming a military alliance with North Korea. Without Korea, Russia would be left with no other choice but to rely on its neighboring country, China, to realize its bid to propel industrial growth. But Beijing will not help Russia's industrial development as the two nations share thousands of miles of border. Russia, estranged on the world stage, will hardly grow beyond a resource-rich country, just like some of the Middle East kingdoms, rich in resources but failing to achieve long-term economic growth.

3. Unfreezing the Abraham Accords

The most positive foreign policy legacy during Trump administration would be the Middle East breakthrough - a set of treaties negotiated between August and December in 2020 at Trump's behest that normalized relations between Israel and the UAE, Bahrain, Sudan, and Morocco - officially referred to as Abraham Accords. Egypt and Jordan as well expressed their intention to join in. The ultimate goal of the accords is to involve Saudi Arabia and create a united front against Iran. It is a strategy of balancing power between the Israel-Sunni countries coalition (including Saudi) and Shiite Iran. Would this clever strategy be workable?

Iranians are the descendants of the ancient Persians and Iran has always been a hegemon in the region. It has such a strong identity as to have maintained its independence against the Ottoman Empire in its heyday. Modern day Iran has complex and unusual political system in which religious leaders hold authority over all affairs of the state and political leaders derive their legitimacy from the religious background. The 'Islamic Republic' was established after the Islamic Revolution led by Ayatollah Khomeini in 1979. Currently, there are four types of political systems in the world: liberal democracy, communist totalitarianism, monarchy, and Islamic Republic.

The Islamic Republic was created based on the ideology of the Iranian revolution against the ills of Western liberal democracy. European countries had long been under religious control of the Catholic Church, but through the Renaissance and the Reformation, liberal democracy came into being that requires separation of state and religion. Liberal democracy along with market economy have brought freedom and affluence, but also contributed to the decline of religion.

In Asian society ethics and morals are still around in the

form of sayings and proverbs of sages, passed down and spread by the ruling elite. Even after the introduction of capitalism, they constituted the fundamental principles of work ethics for long. This is the basis for so-called Confucian capitalism. On the other hand, in Christian society ethics take God's commands as the rules that define right and wrong. The Ten Commandments, for instance, provide a biblical framework for the ethics and violation of the precepts makes a man face the judgement of God.

Right after the Renaissance and the Reformation, the early freedom of religion was meant to be a freedom to choose between Protestantism and Catholicism. However, Charles Darwin's theory of evolution challenged the idea of Christian creationism, and the ethical foundation of Western society began to disintegrate. In the process of seeking new ethical standards, a set of new philosophical ideas emerged, e.g. empiricism which claims that people should rely on practical experience and experiments as a basis for knowledge; utilitarianism which upholds the greatest happiness of the greatest number; atheism and its kinds, nihilism and existentialism. Along the way the Western society fell into decadence, with moral decay and pleasure-seeking. Disillusioned with moral corruption and disorder, the public turned to the new 'political religions' of fascism and communism. The ascetic moralism of Western society, which had been obstinately puritanical until the 19th century, began to dwindle in the early 20th century and completely fell apart after the two world wars.

The Islamic Republic founded by Khomeini seeks the Western-style development of state while preserving traditional Islamic values. Government leaders are elected by regular elections, but the supreme leader and the Guardian Council has either direct or indirect control of the system in general, not to mention ethics, morality and social order. It is the Iranian version of gradual Westernization movement, previously attempted by Asian countries over 100 years ago, summarized in the slogans like "Eastern ways and Western frames," or "Japanese spirit and Western techniques." Iran has pride in its political system and is on a mission to transplant it to Arab monarchies. This has become a fight over a way of life that goes beyond the religious divide between Shia and Sunni.

Former U.S. President Barack Obama employed engagement policy with Iran by signing on the Joint Comprehensive Plan of Action (JCPOA) in July 2015, but President Trump pulled the U.S. out of the Iran nuclear deal in May 2018. Obama saw engagement and diplomacy as the best options to bring about real and meaningful change in Iran, but the Trump administration viewed that Iran was a viable threat to Middle East as well as the West. President Biden's Iran policy seems to be on the same track with that of the Obama administration. Biden, upon taking office, promised to treat Saudi Arabia as a "pariah" over the murder of Iranian-American journalist Jamal Khashoggi. Since then, the Abraham Accords have made no progress.

Saudi Arabia has a population of 30 million, of whom only 12 million are citizens and the rest are foreign workers. The people of Saudi are ruled by the Al Saud family and have no role in electing or changing their rulers, and tribal conflicts are latent. Saudi Arabia's security concerns are internal rather than external. For the oppressed and dissatisfied class in Saudi Arabia, Iran's political system is very attractive. Iran's Revolutionary Guard Corps is fanning the flames of Islamic internationalism in the Middle East as the Comintern of the Soviet Union advocated world communism in the past. Hamas, Hezbollah, and Houthi rebels are Teheran's potent proxies. This serves as a motive for Saudi Arabia and other

Arab monarchies to form a united front with Israel against the Iranian threat.

Iran is suspected of being complicit in the Israel-Gaza conflict. Israeli attacks on Palestine will make it impossible for Saudi Arabia to go ahead with normalizing relations with Israel. The ongoing hostilities in Gaza is fueling regional instability, but if Trump gets re-elected, the second Trump administration would likely to rekindle the Abraham Accords. That is because the United States needs to get out of the Middle East and focus on Asia. More specifically, it wants to prioritize China as the most important threat.

4. Heading for a New War

In his first term, Trump used tariffs as a negotiating tactic, meant to pressure Beijing to address unfair trade practices. President Biden put his own stamp on the China tariffs of as high as 12.5% to 25% that he inherited from Donald Trump. Whether intended or not, President Biden's interest rate hikes ravaged China's real estate sector, resulting in halving the country's growth rate, once close to

10% per annum to around 5%.

However, China still recorded the world' largest trade surplus of over $800 billion in 2023 with exports of $3.4 trillion and imports of $2.6 trillion. China's share of U.S. imports dropped significantly from 19.2% in 2018 to 14.8% in 2023 but Chinese exports of trade goods to the U.S. amounted to about $506 billion and China's imports from the U.S. were $166.1 billion, recording a trade surplus with the U.S. of $340 billion.

The Biden administration's China de-risking strategy is to curb risks avoiding a clean break, employing "China plus one" strategy in cooperation with Europe to spread out supply chains. In contrast, Trump sees China as a threat and is outspoken about the idea of decoupling economy from China, confirming that he would impose a 60% tariff on Chinese imports if he returns to the White House. He also floats a 10% across-the-border tariff on all U.S. imports.

Biden's China policy is in controlled pace taking meticulous steps, but Trump's second term China policy is tantamount to an embargo. It is clear that a 60% tariff will bring inflation in the United States. Exceptions will be made for imports of American products made in China, such as Apple's iPhones and laptop computers from HP and Dell, but the prices of most Chinese industrial goods inevitably will go up. Tariffs on China could worsen inflation and consumer dissatisfaction would pile up, making interest rate cuts impossible. Given that, could Trump deliver what he is promising to do? Analysts warns that a 60% tariff would be detrimental to U.S. economy and intolerable to American consumers. However, it is nothing compared to the suffering that the Chinese people would go through when the excruciating tariffs take effect.

China's exports to the United States exceeded $800 billion a year during the COVID-19 pandemic and still last year China exported goods and services worth roughly $500 billion to the U.S. What would happen is as clear as day if Washington stopped trading with China. Foreign direct investment in China would come to a halt, and Chinese companies' exports to the United States will dwindle down to zero.

China's colossal manufacturing sector includes a variety of industrial products beyond its EV and smartphone brands that make a splash in the overseas market. As witnessed in Ali, Temu and Shein's penetration into the

Korean market, China makes a plethora of light industrial products such as bicycles, toys, household accessories, and clothing. They are competing with manufacturers in Vietnam, Indonesia, Mexico and El Salvador. The 60% tariffs would be a huge windfall for factories in these regions.

Some well-off Chinese companies could move their operations overseas, but others could face production cutdown or complete shutdown. Either way, it means mass unemployment. Big cities would have an increasing number of homeless people, and rural migrant workers would go back to their home villages, and social unrest would exacerbate. Local governments must provide unemployment benefits to these people, but they can't because their tax revenues plummeted due to the real estate crisis. If the central government does not take action, a large number of people would face hunger, malnutrition and even death. Many fear there could be a repeat of the Venezuela crisis.

The U.S. policy toward China evolves through leadership changes in Washington between the Democratic and Republican parties. Trump, in his first term, wielded tariffs to slam China, and on top of that, Biden added high interest rates, and Trump aims at hitting China's low value-added industries with tariffs equivalent to an embargo if he wins a second term in office. Japan started the Pacific War in 1941 in response to the U.S. embargo. The beginning of de facto U.S.-China war is looming ahead.

5. What Lies Beyond the Tariff War

In some ways, the 60% tariff on Chinese goods is a good news for Korean companies in competition in the U.S. market. Even though policy uncertainty is on the rise with the unstrained Trump's second term proposals like repealing the Inflation Reduction Act and ending the electric vehicle mandate, Korean companies already have competitive advantage in the EV, battery, and semiconductor markets. Even better, big market players are relatively better positioned to adapt to changes. Some chaos and confusion are expected in the short run if a China hardliner Trump returns to the White House. But in terms of the bottom-line, it will turn out to be in favor of Korean companies.

If so, what about the universal 10% tariff? Will Korea-U.S. alliance remain intact? We can get a clue about how the future will unfold from Trump's MAGA (Make America Great Again) movement and J.D. Vance who was recently tapped for vice-presidential candidate.

J.D. Vance grew up in the small industrial community of Middletown, Ohio, in the foothills of Appalachia. He was raised by his grandparents. His grandfather worked at the Armco Steel mill, but lost his job when the steel mill shut down in the 1970s as Japan emerged as a major player in the international steel market. Armco was merged with Kawasaki Steel, and the town with a population of about 40,000 fell into dreadful poverty and despair. Vance's mother didn't have a decent education in the deprived family and slid into the addiction to alcohol and drugs through her unstable and unhappy relationships with men. Vance was taken to live with his grandmother.

Vance's grandmother who was poor but strong-minded encouraged him to work hard and do well in school. She refused to allow young Vance to succumb to the cycle of poverty and worked tirelessly to give her grandchildren a pathway out of the despondent, working-class Middletown. With the support and encouragement of his grandmother, Vance, a hillbilly young man from the town with no college student ever, attended Yale Law school. After graduating, he began his career as a lawyer and a venture capitalist in California for years.

It came as a great shock to Vance when he first encountered a typical WASP culture during his time in marine corps, in college and then in the business world of California, that was completely different from the rural Ohio town where he had grown up. He was deeply impressed by the WASP virtues that include a spirit of personal austerity, being family-oriented, and strong sense of responsibility. They honor donating money to the less fortunate on Christmas day rather than grabbing at their own gifts. There are no drunkards, drug addicts, and domestic violence, rancorous fights he used to see in Middletown. None in their neighborhood lie to government officers to get welfare benefits.

In the United States there are two races entirely different. I'm not talking about whites, blacks, or Hispanics. The one is those who are healthy, determined and independent, and the other is the lazy, hedonistic and dependent. This divide derived from the global strategy of the United States after World War II. To aid war-torn Europe and Asia, American elites pushed for opening the market at such speed and scope that American workers could not withstand. Traditional manufacturing base or Rust Belt in the Midwestern United states, including Chicago, Detroit, and Pittsburgh began to falter facing the emergence of Japanese competitors in the 1970s, and collapsed completely when China joined the global market. Vance's grandparents and his mother were victimized by the industrial decline, but Vance was fortunate to have his grandmother who encouraged him to rise above.

J.D. Vance is the embodiment of the MAGA movement. The MAGA movement is, in fact, a commitment to bring back the American Dream. It is not just for blue-collar whites. It is a movement to create a country where hillbillies from Kentucky and Ohio, not only the elites in San Francisco and New York, can have a good life if they work hard.

American working class rallied to embrace MAGA, and Trump stormed his way into the Republican establishment. However, the Democratic Party has been the traditional home of labor unions. The Democratic Party will respond to this movement in some way and bipartisan progress could be made in the process. Its current target is China, but Japan and Korea will be the next in time. The 10% universal tariff is just a first step.

6. A Silver Lining in a Gloomy Outlook

Just as the Ukraine war permanently damaged the economic models of Germany and Russia, the MAGA movement could be an overture of the economic models of Japan and Korea coming to an end. Japan produces twice as much as it consumes and the surplus is exported overseas. Further, Korea produces three times more than the domestic consumption, as the 70% of trade dependence stands for.

While grappling with the great appreciation of the Yen following the Plaza Agreement, Japanese companies successfully executed its localization strategy in export markets. Japan's economy is three times larger than South Korea's, but Korea is inching closer to overtake Japan in total exports contrarily demonstrates Japan's high level of localization. Korea has exported its way to prosperity, but in the era of post-globalization, excessive trade surplus is not necessarily good for the country's economy.

More and more countries are moving towards closed economies and global trade is increasingly under attack on the high seas. The population is on the decrease, the industrial workforce is shrinking faster, and companies are becoming less and less competitive. Except for a handful of branded products and high-tech products, trade barriers such as tariffs reduce imports of intermediate goods and low-tech products. Setting up foreign subsidiaries is an alternative, but even large corporations, except for Samsung and Hyundai, find it difficult to build factories in the United States and Europe.

Factories in Korea may close just as Ohio lost thousands of factories over the last decade, and Ulsan and Pohang, home to the large industrial cluster, may go down the same path with Detroit or Pittsburgh. Futurist George Friedman and geopolitical strategist Peter Zeihan predict that the post-globalization could prove to be the darkest era for Korea and suggest that Korea should strengthen partnership with Japan to pull through. Will there be a way out?

On June 3, President Yoon unveiled the Blue Whale Project, the first exploratory drilling of the potential gas and oil field in the East Sea. It sounds like a far-fetched idea as yet, but if Korea becomes an oil-producing country, it will be an opportunity to overhaul the export-led growth model that Korea has employed since the 1960s.

Korea exports commodities and with the export earnings it imports oil and raw materials to run its factories, feeding the entire country with the added-value created in the process. Roughly speaking, Korea's domestic demand is a part of production structures primarily towards export-led growth, and its financial industry is built on the large export surpluses.

If the East Sea oil and gas field becomes operational, Korea can cut down exports significantly, and does not need to be obsessed with trade surplus. And it can import iPhones, EVs, aircrafts, and agricultural products in proportion to exports. If factories in America's Rust Belt are running again, Korea could be one of their biggest buyers.

The economic value of 14 billion barrels of oil production is estimated to be worth $ 1.6 trillion, which in turn would offset depleting tax revenues when the nation is reeling from shrinking population. If the oil revenue of $ 1.6 trillion is invested into sovereign wealth funds, it could provide an extra source of capital with the dividend payments of about $ 81 billion every year. It is close to the annual welfare expenditure of the Korean government, which currently amounts to around $ 88 billion.

A word of caution: Korea must stay financially sound and be ready for potential industrial restructuring that is looming over the horizon. Bailout funds should be set aside in case the country's manufacturing base shrinks due to a decrease in exports. In terms of debt management, Korea is not in the same shoe as the U.S. and European countries, since Korean won (KRW) is not a key currency like the dollar and the euro. Possibly, the East Sea oil field might become one of the financial sources for the upcoming industrial restructuring.

Korea-Japan relation should also improve. The two countries' relationship has been on a bumpy road due to unsolved historical disputes and bitter national sentiments towards each other. As a matter of fact, Korea lacks leverage over Japan. Japanese companies have transformed their supply chain structures toward vertical integration ranging from raw materials, parts, and equipment to high-tech and finished products. Japan is the fourth largest economy in the world with financial assets exceeding $2 trillion. Moreover, Japan has the world's second largest naval power to protect its maritime shipping and trade without relying on the United States.

Korea's East Sea oil and gas field may deliver Korea the

much-coveted leverage over Japan. It is much cheaper and safer to connect the Osaka-Nagoya industrial zone with an offshore pipeline from the East Sea rather than mining for natural gas in Siberia, Russia. It is also good for carbon neutrality. Korea's gas field would be a fluke for Japanese industries. Stability on the Korean peninsula is essential to Japan's national interests, so Japanese navy will be more than ready to help secure the seas for maritime trade.

If Trump returns to the White House, the tension between the U.S. and China will escalate and the situation in Northeast Asia may change dramatically. The big difference between Trump and Biden is that Trump is looking at the global picture beyond China's borders. The United States' global strategy towards 'deglobalization' will ultimately have a significant impact on the Korean economy.

The economic model that has been driving Korea for the last 60 years is on its last legs. Amidst the gloomy outlook, the exploratory drilling plan of the potential gas field in the East Sea comes as a whisper saying 'Don't give up. Keep going!' May Heaven help us and our endeavors in East Sea lead to handsome reward.

PART 3
Changes in Industries

Global Economy under Geopolitical Change

A New Sweeping Wave of Antitrust Aimed at Big Tech[1)]

1. The Rise of Big Business

1) American Civil War

The United Sates was an agricultural country prior to the Civil War (1861~1865). Its main export was agricultural products and most of manufactured goods were imported from the UK. The northern US, a temperate zone, grew staple crops like wheat and maize, and its manufacturing industry was nothing but small-scaled craft except for a few textile factories. In the meantime, the subtropical South mass-produced cash crops like tobacco, cotton, and sugar cane. Then the American Civil War broke out over the expansion of slavery into newly acquired Midwest, revealing the fact that the North and South were two different regimes.

Slavery, now considered inhumane crimes, had to do with commercial agriculture of the southern region that

---

1) This column was published on September 3, 2021.

required labor force all year round. In the temperate zone that had four marked seasons slaves became idle labor force after harvest until the next year's sowing season, and farm owners were obliged to give them a shelter and food. That was one of the primary reasons for the early abolishment of slavery and why contract wage system was widely adopted in the North. On the other hand, in the subtropical region where year-round growing and harvesting is possible, slavery was more efficient for plantations. The south even chose a war to maintain the system intact. In short, the North and South were two irreconcilable, very different regimes.

The North won the war, opening an era of Republican dominance. The Republican party founded by Lincoln was an awkward alliance of former members of the Whig Party, Federalists, anti-immigrants against the massive influx of Irish workers, and abolitionists. However, the majority was ex-Whigs who were oriented towards pro-development and pro-business. Supported by emerging middle class including the northern farmers and city businessmen the Republican Party had dominated Washington for almost 70 years after the war until the Great Depression devastated the country.

With the pro-development politicians in power, the

Transcontinental Railroad which President Abraham Lincoln had proposed during the war was completed in 1869, connecting the United States from East to West by rail. Being politically stable and geographically unified, the country began to see markets growing bigger and businesses thriving. The 40 years after the war were a period of exponential economic growth - the Guilded Age as Mark Twain depicted.

As corporations started to expand their business across the continent, it gave rise to big businesses. Andrew Carnegie in steel, John D. Rockefeller in oil refining, Jay Gould in railroad business and many other young entrepreneurs came to the market. Among them, John Pierpont Morgan, a man of good bearing, brought a wind of change to the Wall Street. While other financiers were complacent with interest and fee income, he restructured America's railroads and steel industry, building his fortune. During the bank panic of 1907, he even took the role of the central bank to stabilize the financial market. These young successful entrepreneurs became an object of envy and jealousy and were labelled as 'Robber Barons'. Rockefeller's Standard Oil was at the center of the rising sentiment against big businesses.

2) The World's First Multinational Corporation- Standard Oil Co.

The oil industry was founded by the U.S. and kerosene was invented in the country, too. Whale oil used in oil lamps and coal oil were expensive and inefficient. Since Edwin Drake became the first American to successfully drill for oil in Titusville, Pennsylvania in 1859, it took only 10 years for kerosene to dominate the global market, not to mention the US market. Product from one U.S. state replaced the lighting market across the world.

The emerging oil industry, however, came with a plethora of problems. Drillers rushed to oil fields in Pennsylvania and soon over-drilling became a major problem. As oil fields were connected underground, whoever came first could get the most. Over-drilled excess oil was discarded, leaving the oil fields in a mess. Oil price plummeted. Even the once flourishing city of Pithole rapidly declined to a ghost city in just one year with the depletion of oil wells. Scientists warned oil would be depleted in less than a decade.

Refiners were another problem. The skyrocketing price of refineries caused speculation. Farmers sold their land that they had acquired under the Homestead Act, which allowed people to stake a claim of 160 acres of land free-of-charge, and then bought refineries in poor condition. The speculative market was swamped with lies and frauds. Bad refineries produced low quality kerosene with a large quantity of impurities, which was at high risk of terrible explosions. In fact, in the mid-1870s, the explosions claimed the lives of about 5,000 to 6,000 people a year.

Transporting oil was a challenge, too. Barrels filled with oil in the mountainous regions of Pennsylvania were loaded onto flatboats and then floated down the Allegheny River. That was not a sustainable solution. Standardized storage, vast drop-off points with easy accessibility and cost-effective delivery system were required on land and water.

It was Rockefeller who solved all these problems. Rockefeller was not a man of good bearing like J.P. Morgan nor eloquent as Carnegie, but he meticulously and quietly dominated the oil refining industry. Rockefeller couldn't go to college due to his father's opposition, but he used his early background in accounting to quantify every business-related equipment with rulers, scales, and numbers. He was completely different from others who were speculative, buying up oil well sites, mobilizing drillers, and aiming for quick profit.

From the beginning, Rockefeller instinctively realized that centralized and integrated management of the 'visible hand[2]' was essential to eliminate uncertainty in the oil business which was reckless and wasteful over-drilling. During the late 1860s and early 1870s, he acquired regional oil refineries, oil pipelines, storage tanks, loading docks, oil tankers, logistics companies, and coastal wharf facilities, and formed an alliance with the Erie Railway and New York Central Railway to secure the lowest price for rail transportation. Rockefeller strictly kept his business deals in secret, so no one knew what was going on for over a decade.

At the time it was illegal for a company to own a company, so Rockefeller and his partners innovated a first-of-its-kind trust, where they issued trust certificates and swapped their individual holdings for shares in the trust[3], building an oil empire (1882). The shareholders of the acquired company became members of the trust

---

2) The "visible hand" is an economic concept invented by Alfred Chandler, professor of business history at Harvard Business School, that contrasts with what Adam Smith referred to as the invisible hand of market forces. It refers to centralized management of big business.

3) The term, 'trust' comes from the cartel system of the Standard Oil where they swapped certificates of trust, replacing the term 'monopoly'.

committee. The trust was managed and coordinated by a set of committees including Domestic Marketing Committee, Export Trade Committee, Manufacturing Committee, Human Resources Committee, Pipeline Committee, Transportation Committee, Lubricating Oil Committee, and Production Committee.

As technology was shared and quality management was secured, explosions disappeared. Consumer oil prices fell nearly to 10%. As prices fell, more people bought oil products and cash poured in. Businesses with the trust certificates were happy with the large dividends. Standard Oil Co. expanded its market to Europe and even to the Far East beyond the United States and became the world's first multinational company. It alone controlled 90% of the global market. This monopoly lasted until Nobel-Rothschild cartel was formed in Baku, Russia, and Marcus Samuel (1853-1927) founded Shell Transport and Trading Company in Indonesia.

The huge success of the oil trust brought a surge in this new type of business organization. Corporate trusts were formed across the whole spectrum of economy ranging from railways, steel, meat-packing, telecommunications, tobacco, sewing machines, and food, and by the early

1900s more than 300 trusts were formed. This caused concerns over monopolies.

2. Antitrust Waves

1) The first wave: 1901 ~ The Great Depression

The Sherman Antitrust Act, the first federal law to regulate companies was passed in 1890, but businessmen did not care. Until then corporate law had been a matter of a state authority and not on the federal agenda. It was difficult to determine in the world of cut-throat business competition what constitutes "restriction of trade," "significant reduction in competition," and "monopoly" as defined in the Antitrust Act as the US has been traditionally a common law country.

Americans had mixed feelings about monopoly. Big corporations in steel, oil, railroads, and telecommunications were taken as the embodiment of the industrial advancement of the nation. People thought that large-scale production facilities and distribution networks were needed for these companies to be globally competitive.

They took pride in that U.S. Steel was competing with Britain for dominance of the global steel market and that startups like AT&T operated the world's largest telephone network. Consumers were satisfied with the pleasant service provided by Union Pacific, which operated the transcontinental railroad. Beef was made available and affordable to the middle classes as Swift & Co. invented refrigerated railcars to carry frozen meat to the cities. As a result, people got healthier, and children grew taller.

At the same time, however, dissatisfaction was growing bigger, too. Big businesses demand constant change on the part of intermediaries, wholesalers, local businesses, and those involved in the acquired company. In the process of business restructuring, frictional unemployment increased, and small local merchants were pushed into a corner. The wealth gap between employers and employees widened, and large-scale labor disputes took place. Conflict between office workers and manual workers intensified, and crimes against strangers increased. Families were torn apart in search of work. The speed of life was going increasingly faster, and people felt tired.

The media took notice of the underlying public dissatisfaction over big businesses and began to report on the popular sentiment. Ethics and high moral standards required for politicians and public officials began to be imposed on businessmen. That is to say, ethics have been incorporated into businesses. Ida Minerva Tarbel (1857-1944), a female writer for McClure's Magazine, began a meticulous investigation on the awkward and shady practices of Rockefeller and Standard Oil and published a total of19 articles of exposé of Standard Oil from 1902 to 1903. She became a great journalist who developed modern investigative reporting techniques. Upton Sinclair, in the meantime, in his 1906 novel *The Jungle*, depicted the inhumane conditions that workers suffered in the large-scale meat industry. His descriptions on wretched reality of immigrant workers shocked and galvanized readers. The novel helped him make a political debut.

On the back of the public sentiment against big business, progressives gained momentum. As corporate mergers swept across the United States and the number of trusts soared, antitrust became a major political issue. William Jennings Bryan (1860-1925), a young and passionate orator ran twice in a row as the Democratic presidential candidate, at the age of 36 and 40, against Republican president William McKinley (in office 1897-1901). During his nationwide campaign tour, he advocated for protecting consumer rights and social justice, improving working conditions, and curbing the power of large corporations.

Vilified by journalists, intellectuals, and progressive politicians, businessmen treated them as socialists and placed their hopes on the Republican Party, which had led the era of prosperity. Rockefeller made a generous donation to McKinley, saying "Republican politicians are reliable." McKinley won the election twice against Bryan, to the relief of big businesses, but he was assassinated six months after being re-elected. The young Vice President Theodore Roosevelt (in office 1901-1909) succeeded him, but he was a maverick Republican.

The hero of the Spanish American War was nominated to be vice president by McKinley, but Roosevelt was bored with the job as it had not much to do. Then, six months later, Mckinley was assassinated, making him the youngest president, age 43, in U.S. history. The young president was an outsider and had no support base within the Republican party. He determined to put his agenda into action, despite the opposition from the party - regulating large corporations. He refused to let his vigorous courses of action be delayed by Republican Congress and ordered the Department of Justice to pursue his agenda.

Roosevelt's legal weapon of choice was the Sherman Anti-trust Act, which had been rarely invoked. The Roosevelt administration sued successfully to break up 43 trusts for 7-year period from 1902 including railroads, steel, oil refineries, meatpacking, and food. Standard Oil's indictment in November 1906 was the at the peak of the government's attack on monopolies. Unlike other trusts, kerosene was one of the most widely used consumer goods, so American consumers felt the heat.

The Supreme Court weighed in. It applied the so-called "rule of reason' interpretation of vague provisions of the Act. What is reasonable or not? The Supreme Court ruled the US steel was not a monopoly as its 50% of market share was in line with the rule of reason, but Standard Oil with its 90% of market share was a monopoly. Presumably, it was because Andrew Carnegie, founder of Carnegie Steel which would go on to form the basis of US Steel, was loved by the public for his generous philanthropy, but Rockefeller of Standard Oil was vilified and hated by many following the investigative report by the female writer Tarbel. Supreme Court justices had no choice but to be influenced by the public opinion.

In 1911, Standard Oil was broken up into 33 regional companies, including Exxon (New Jersey), Mobil (New York), Sohio (Ohio), and SoCal (California), followed by the dissolution of 20 other trusts. Ironically, dozens of American conglomerates were dismembered under the Republican rule that had led America's long-term prosperity, by the Republican rebel Theodore Roosevelt who accidentally came into office. Roosevelt earned a reputation as a Trust Buster. The breakup of trusts lasted until the Great Depression of 1929.

2) The Second Wave: Postwar ~ 1980

The World War I has changed modern Europe, and it was the Great Depression that has changed America. The political landscape of the United States has been shifted. Before the Depression U.S. politics had been dominated by the Republican Party which was almost identical to the pre-civil war Whigs. In the face of the historic economic downturn, the Democratic Party became more progressive ideologically and inclined towards government intervention. When the charming and gentle politician, Franklin D. Roosevelt (FDR, in office 1931-1945) campaigned for presidency calling for the federal government to help "the forgotten men[4]" at the bottom of the economic pyramid, he won support from some intellectuals skeptical of capitalism and the urban working class. The Democratic Party, aligned with white Southerners, significantly broadened their appeal in big cities and seized their electoral edge. Put on the defensive and with no clear-cut candidates within the party, the conservative Republicans, desperately turned to Dwight D. Eisenhower, a war hero, and barely kept afloat. For about half a century from FDR, the Democratic Party had led the U.S. politics and could push their progressive agenda with little opposition from the Republicans until Ronald Reagan came to help the Republican Party to win elections.

The World War II, in the meantime, devasted most of industrial facilities in Europe and Japan, leaving the United States stand tall as the world's only industrialized country. Progressive camps in the United States began to raise their criticism against the anti-monopoly, which had been silenced during the Great Depression and the war. Of course, trusts had been dismembered and there

---

4) The concept has become famous after Roosevelt used the phrase in the 1932 radio address to describe the poor men who were unemployed and neglected, calling for plans to support them.

were no conglomerates created from merger, but this had not been the case for the high-tech industry. Four new giants emerged in the electronics industry: AT&T, RCA, IBM, and XEROX. They were built upon their technological prowess and dominated the world's telecommunication, TV, computer, and copier markets beyond the United States. They were not exempt from antitrust charges, but the authorities took a different approach.

From the experiences in the 1910s and 1920s, anti-monopoly authorities learned that breaking up the trusts had limitations. In fact, companies split from the Standard Oil in 1911 were better off as the dissolution of Standard Oil stabilized oil markets split by region and most of all, demands for gasoline growing exponentially thanks to the booming automobile industry. Rockefeller, though he stepped down from the throne of the oil empire, became the wealthiest man in the US history as the stock price went up. This raised a question about the effectiveness of the antitrust authorities' way of dealing with monopolies. So, the U.S. government took a different approach to these four big businesses.

In 1958, the Department of Justice forced RCA, IBM, and AT&T to license out their patents. And again in 1975 the same measure was taken against XEROX, which had been dominating the global document management market with its plain paper copier in 1959. DOJ's logic behind the measure was that big companies should license out their patents to make the technology available to competitors. This is the first case that the issue of 'monopoly' was taken as more important than 'patent' in the U.S., a country traditionally known for patent protection.

Holding a monopoly on telephone network, AT&T licensed only its semiconductor technology owned by the Bell Labs. IBM, too, licensed its old patents, but quickly turned to the personal computer (PC) market with the iconic IBM System/360, ushering in an era of computer compatibility. The DOJ's anti-trust measure prompted the patents and technical manpower of Bell Labs and IBM to flow outside, and it laid a foundation for Silicon Valley's startups such as Intel, Fairchild Semiconductor, Texas Instruments, Micron, Motorola, Apple, and Microsoft. America's semiconductor and computer industries thrived.

However, the fates of RCA and XEROX were different. RCA was an empire, controlling the electronics industry until the 1950s with revenue from radio/TV sales, radio package technology transfer, and NBC broadcasting. In particular, its 3-color vacuum tubes, which allowed many Americans to watch television both in color or black and white were an outstanding and unmatched technology. Although RCA's technologies were made available to U.S. companies under the pressure of DOJ, they did not show much interest in the color TV market and focused on manufacturing profitable, single products such as vacuum tubes and electronic parts. Instead, foreign companies rushed in.

David Sarnoff, RCA's CEO, in the meantime, turned his attention to overseas markets, where he could receive royalties for technology transfer from companies like Philips in Europe and Japanese companies. They were granted unlimited access to the RCA technology in return for loyalty fee, and RCA earned 200 to 300 million dollars a year from royalties alone. With the technological boon coming across the Pacific, start-up companies in Japan such as Sony, Matsushita, Sharp, and Sanyo grew fast and big.

In 1965, RCA formulated two strategies that would have a profound impact on the future of the company and the American electronics industry. The first was to challenge IBM in the computer market, and the second was to transform RCA into a giant conglomerate. RCA, as if enchanted by Siren, succumbed to the temptation of computer and the curse of big business.

IBM, however, with its development of new products at the speed of light, was a 'moving target'. RCA's challenge to IBM ended in failure, leaving a loss of $500 million. In the meantime, aiming at becoming a giant conglomerate, RCA acquired 'Random House', a publishing company, 'Arnold Palmer', a golf brand, and 'Hertz', a car rental business. However, its overstretching business diversification was unsuccessful and drained out the company's finance.

XEROX, a market dominant with global market share of close to 90%, licensed out up to 1,700 patents, earning royalties on technology transfer. However, it never expected that Seiko Epson and Canon, Japanese companies came out with compact copiers with a catchphrase of "Small is beautiful". A Japanese company acquired a controlling stake of XEROX, putting an end to its market dominance. DOJ's antitrust measures brought down RCA and XEROX, and helped Japanese companies grow instead. Worse still, it destroyed the entire consumer electronics industry of the U.S., far from intensifying market competition. This led to a call within the country for understanding what went wrong and how to fix them.

Robert Bork, an anti-trust officer under the Nixon administration in the 1970s, criticized the United States antitrust laws in his 1978 book, *The Antitrust Paradox,* saying "The only legitimate goal of antitrust should be to maximize consumer welfare." He claimed that one should not judge a smaller firm, or a less efficient competitor as "worth protecting".

Ronald Reagan, taking office as president in 1981, embraced Bork's argument, and the government stopped engaging in large-scale mergers and acquisitions unless consumer welfare is reduced. Since the 1980s, mergers and acquisitions took place in almost all areas of the United States, including pharmaceuticals, aviation, steel, automobiles, cargo transportation, seed, chemical, and telecommunication industries, and all of them were approved by antitrust authorities. It laid a groundwork for Microsoft building up a software empire, and creation of online giants such as Google, Amazon, Facebook, and Apple (GAFA).

3. The Third Wave

1) Global Fight over Big Tech

Recently, the antitrust debate over Big Tech is growing fierce. No doubt that the Tech Giants have opened a whole new world to mankind which is convenient and pleasant, but it is also true that the platform companies are heading towards monopoly. This column is not going to delve into the ongoing, complicated economic and legal debates over how they are doing their business, whether consumer welfare is taken priority, or whether competition is highly restrained. However, the need for regulating Big Tech has already been raised in various forms, not only in the United States but also in countries across the world. We need to take a step back and look at these issues more carefully.

First, there has been little regulation for Big Tech in the United States for the past 40 years, and the regulatory movement has largely come from overseas. Europe, known for its social democratic regulations, has failed to produce world-class online companies. It has been criticizing GAFA and calling for regulation to protect the regional market. EU, trying to protect the regional industries, and the U.S. wanting to protect its own businesses, clashed.

During the Trump administration EU countries tried to charge American tech giants a 2~3% levy on digital revenue, prompting threats from the U.S. government to impose 25% of retaliatory tariffs on European imports. In addition, EU demanded payment from Google and Facebook that has encroached on the media market, in exchange for using their content. In February 2021, the Australian government proposed the 'News Media Bargaining Code' forcing Google and Facebook to pay for news, and France's antitrust watchdog slapped a $593 million fine on Google in April of the same year for failing to comply the regulator's orders to conduct talks with the country's leading news publishers.

As an alternative to the EU's digital services taxes, the Biden administration has made a proposal to allow the tech companies a 10 percent profit margin but impose a 20-30% tax on any profit above that level. What the Biden administration is aiming for is the introduction of a global minimum corporate tax of at least 15%. Biden, who needs tax increases, is planning to bring U.S. conglomerates who have moved their headquarters abroad in search of lower corporate tax rates back to their home country.

Ireland, Hungary, and Estonia are three lowest corporate

tax countries in the EU, and they are opposing the minimum tax. However, as the influence of the trio within the EU is not large, the global minimum tax is expected to be adopted without difficulty. This means that an "excess profit tax" will soon replace the digital services taxes. In addition, the U.S. Department of Commerce is suggesting digital giant's paying for news content be implemented after a more extensive study, and this suggestion could be officially made to Australia, France, and other countries. So we need to watch it closely.

In the end, the foreign government's regulatory move on Big Tech is nothing more than the EU's mercantilist policy, and GAFA is not very worried as they know they will be ultimately protected under the umbrella of the U.S. government. Facebook refused to pay foreign governments for news content and declared that it would block access to news content. However, the problem lies in what is going on in the U.S. government.

2) Biden Administration's Antitrust Moves

The movement of the U.S. government is signaling a big swing. In July 2021 President Biden signed on an executive order on 'Prompting Competition in America', saying, "We're now 40 years into the experiment of allowing giant corporations to accumulate more and more power. What have we gotten from it? Less growth, weakened investment, fewer small businesses."

Biden appointed Lina Khan, 32-year-old young law school professor, to head the Federal Trade Commission and Jonathan Kanter to head the Justice Department's Antitrust Division. Lina Kahn has been known for her criticism against Amazon since her days in Yale law school, and Jonathan Kanter is also a known Google critic. Reminiscent of Ida Tarbel, who took on Standard Oil, Lina Khan follows the philosophies of Louis Brandeis (1916-1939, Supreme Court Justice), who was dubbed as a "People's Lawyer".

"Size, we are told, is not a crime," Brandeis wrote. "But size may, at least, become noxious by reason of the means through which it is attained or the uses to which it is put." And he inspired the Clayton Antitrust Act to be passed by the Congress in 1914. The Act clarifies the abstract Sherman Act and restricts unfair practices and business combinations. Brandeis believed a democratic society should include workers' right and freedom to negotiate with their employers. This freedom applies equally to other economic agents, so that suppliers can negotiate with retailers, retailers with suppliers, and farmers with bankers. To this end, the market must be teeming with as many participants as can be.

The Neo-Brandeis movement advocated by Lina Khan manifests itself with a slogan, "Big is bad. Don't let large firms merge. The end." This, replacing Robert Bork's emphasis on consumer welfare, aims at various objectives such as protecting SMEs and small business owners and solving social problems. These objectives are hard to be quantified and can vary from time to time according to the social agenda. Already, Lina Khan has barred Amazon from acquiring MGM Studios for $8.5 billion, putting the brakes on Big Tech's M&A efforts.

3) Backfire from the Bipartisan Antitrust Reforms

Many experts predict that the FTC's new leadership will be challenged by the Congress and the Supreme Court, not to mention by large corporations armed with money and best lawyers. Microsoft is one of the most cited cases.

In 1991, Microsoft was sued for trying to monopolize

the personal computer market and faced the Clinton administration's order to break up the company into two entities in 1998. But a federal appeals court reversed the breakup order in 2002 during Bush administration. The antitrust legal battle against Microsoft continued for over 12 years through three presidencies. The case shows that Robert Bork's philosophy of consumer welfare was kept alive at least theoretically, but more frankly speaking, the U.S. administration and the Supreme Court agreed on a settlement with Microsoft in favor of the national interest of the United States.

Nevertheless, the year of 2021 will mark a milestone in the history of antitrust. On June 11, a bipartisan group of lawmakers in the U.S. House of Representatives introduced four antitrust bills[5] aimed at reining in the power of the Big Tech. The Democratic and Republican parties agreed to chip away at the power of big tech companies that they fear have grown too big.

Democrats believe that Facebook and Twitter removed

---

5) The American Innovation and Choice Online Act, The Platform Competition and Opportunity Act, The Augmenting Compatibility and Competition by Enabling Service Switching Act (ACCESS Act), The Ending Platform Monopolies Act

and censored Trump's Russia scandal as fake news during the 2016 presidential election, which eventually led to his victory. Republicans, in the meantime, suspect that Big Tech is censoring the accounts held by leading politicians and is making up the biggest source of Democrat campaign contributions. Just as Democrats in the past viewed Rockefeller and Carnegie a pain in the neck as they gave large donations to Republican Party, now both parties are set to take under control the substantial power of Big tech that could influence their political future.

It is unclear whether the sweeping antitrust overhaul will be implemented or not, as GAFA is armed with the best lawyers and lobbying powers and the Supreme Court has become decidedly more conservative during Trump's presidency. However, when Biden took office, Congress and the administration got united to take on GAFA's monopoly power. In the first wave of anti-monopoly (1901 ~ the Great Depression), the progressive party within the Republican Party, formed by Theodore Roosevelt, spearheaded in dismantling the trusts. And in the second wave of antitrust (post war ~ 1980), progressives licensed out patents held by cutting-edge tech companies. The past 160 years of history since the Civil War tells that large corporations cannot win against Congress and the government.

The third antitrust wave will soon sweep across the world. Recently, South Korean parliament approved a bill that will ban major app store operators from mandating developers to only use their in-app payment systems to process the sale of digital products and services. Korea has a number of large tech companies too. That is why it needs keep an eye on this new wave of antitrust movement.

References

1. 『The Prize Part I』, Daniel Yergin
   It chronicles history of the global petroleum industry and depicts the rise of Standard Oil from an objective perspective.

2. 『The Tycoons』, Charles R. Morris
   It gives a good account of the life of the tycoons such as Carnegie, Rockefeller, Gould and Morgan during the Gilded Age.

3. 『Inventing the Electronic Century』, Alfred Chandler
   It traces the history of the consumer electronics and computer businesses in different countries and helps readers understand the demise of RCA.

4. 『The Four: The Hidden DNA of Amazon, Apple, Facebook, and Google』, Scott Galloway
   It gives insightful depiction of GAFA's staggering success and its dark side.

5. 『Taking on the Trust』, Steve Weinberg

It is about the epic battle of Ida Tarbell against John D. Rockefeller and Standard Oil in reference to Tarbell's investigative reporting.

Europe's Descent into Deindustrialization[1]

1. Two Major Events

1) Aftermath of Nord Stream Gas Leaks

Russia's shutdown of Nord Stream .I II, gas pipelines directly connected to Germany, at the end of last September has significant political and economic implications on the global level. It means that Germany has lost its ability to decide its destiny.

Germany has two overland gas pipelines that run through Poland and Ukraine respectively, and the subsea Nord Stream pipeline. Poland, which sees Russia as an enemy has closed the pipeline soon after Russia's war against Ukraine broke out, and the Ukrainian line is still in operation. As the subsea Nord Stream pipeline was disabled, Germany is left with only the overland Ukrainian pipeline, putting its future of gas supply at the hands of Ukraine.

---

1) This column was published on December 21, 2022.

Natural gas is by far the most important energy source for Germany's industries, but its impact on the Russian economy is small. Natural gas accounts for only 8% of the Russian economy, so shutdown of some gas pipelines is not going to hurt the Russian economy badly. On the other hand, the cutting off the supply of inexpensive natural gas from Russia poses a fatal threat to Europe, especially detrimental to the manufacturing-oriented German economy.

As long as hostilities between Russia and Ukraine continue, there is no chance that Germany's gas supply will return to pre-war conditions. Now Germany is forced to be on its way to cut its dependence on Russian energy by the end of 2027 in compliance with the EU plan to quit Russian fossil fuels. The world is wondering about what the future that it brings would be like.

2) Russian Oil Price Cap

Russia's oil and gas industry accounted for around 40% of the country's gross domestic product (GDP). Rising oil prices have made Russia's oil and gas revenues jump even higher, so Russia has no problem in making payment for imports and financing its war. In order to put pressure on Russia, EU must put the brakes on Russia's oil industry. This is why it is putting a cap on Russian oil prices for $60 per barrel.

Microeconomists say oligopolies are prone to collapse. Cartels of three or four oligopolistic suppliers often fall apart and what will happen to a buyers' cartel of more than 30 countries? Will the countries depending daily on Russian oil that makes up 10% of the world's oil supply, be able to hold the $60 price cap in the face of Russia's threat to oil cutoff?

The first key to the question lies in geography. In order for Russia to supply oil at international prices, it must cut off pipelines and transport it by sea. To ward off the EU's price cap, Russia has added 90 scrappy tankers over the past few months to ship its crude oil. However, Russia has only two shipping routes, one passing through the Baltic Sea to the Atlantic Ocean and the other through the Bosporus to the Mediterranean Sea. The Baltic Sea is surrounded by NATO members, and the Bosporus Strait is the sovereign national territory of Turkey. Turkey is taking neutral stance on the Russia-Ukraine war, but is a member of NATO after all. Closing off the Baltic Sea and the Bosporus would put Russian tankers to a halt.

The second key is marine insurance. The International Convention requires oil tankers to be covered by maritime cargo insurance and the global maritime insurance market is dominated by the G7 countries, primarily by the UK and the US. Russian oil tanker fleet, obliged to be prepared for maritime accidents and abide by environmental regulations, cannot sail without western insurance. Russia and Saudi Arabia are dominant players in the global oil cartel, while Britain and the US dominate the global financial markets. It remains to be seen which is stronger.

The only viable option for Russia now, is to stop oil production and cut off supplies. However, when Russia stops oil production in its frosty regions, the facilities will be frozen and soon become inoperable. Out of Russia's daily production of 10 million barrels, 6 million barrels are for exports. But with the Europe's ban on Russian oil, Russia cannot keep the huge amount of excess oil in store, nor dump it into the sea. As the oil price cap is likely to be implemented, Russia is in a dilemma and a red sign is turned on for its economy.

2. Europe's Industrial Environments Going Harsh

1) Conditions for Prosperity

Approximately 35 million, or 15% of the labor force are employed in manufacturing industry in Europe. Germany takes up 27% of the EU industrial production, Italy 16% and France 11%. In particular, Germany, the fourth largest economy in the world and the largest in Europe, relies heavily on manufacturing for about 20% of the GDP. This is one of the highest among the G7 countries. Germany's wealth comes mainly from exports and a quarter of its jobs is generated in the export sector.

In the aftermath of reunification in 1989, German economy had suffered dearly with the unemployment rate rising up to 12%, but there were two important momentums before it could enjoy its present prosperity. The first was the launch of the euro in 1999 and the second was the increase in exports to China since the 2010s.

When the launch of the single currency in 1999 invigorated trade within the region and the euro became legal tender in 2002, EU member countries took the impact in a mixed tone in terms of their industrial competitiveness. At its launching, the euro had taken the average value of participating currencies. This had the effect of lowering the product prices of German companies that had used the "strong" Deutsche Mark, at the same time taking away the price competitiveness of southern European businesses that had used the "weak" currencies like the lira and the drachma. Germany's manufacturing industry has gradually taken over Europe, the world's biggest consumer market, with their low-priced products.

The second momentum was offshore exports, notably to China. Since joining the WTO in 2001, China has continued to grow rapidly, and in the 2010s, the explosive growth brought the rise of the middle class in the coastal regions. They bought German luxury cars, and imported reliable German construction machinery in large numbers to build infrastructure, cities, and transportation network.

The German economy is facing many challenges as it is strongly manufacturing-oriented but lags behind in service industries such as finance and big tech. Decreasing number of labor force due to aging population, high wages over 40,000 dollars for GDP per capita, and industrial unions have contributed to creating a rigid wage structure. German companies are subject to one of the strictest environmental regulations and imposed with CO2 emission reduction target. German households pay three times more for electricity than those in France due to their ambitious efforts to concurrently implement energy transition and nuclear phase-out. It is no exaggeration to say that the German manufacturing industry faces unfavorable business conditions in terms of labor, environment, and electricity costs.

The only competitive factor was energy prices. Germany's energy policy, which was in the spirit of Chancellor Willy Brandt's Ostpolitik, has prioritized commercial ties with Russia for more than 20 years, regardless of the ruling party being left or right, from Gerhard Schröder of the Social Democratic Party to Angela Merkel of the CDU. It was a combination of German manufacturing and Russian energy. Germany was able to compete with the United States rich in resources and East Asian countries with cheap labor, thanks to inexpensive Russian gas. It is the Russian energy that has been the source of Germany's competitiveness. Germany has been dominating the world's automotive, machinery, chemical, and optics sectors on the base of thousands of hidden champions, or small but highly successful companies.

2) Collapse of Manufacturing Industry

Germany has been dependent on Russia for 55% of its gas, 50% of its coal and 35% of its oil consumption. Coal and oil are provided at international prices, but the price of Russian natural gas was only 1/3 to 1/2 of that of the US before the Russian-Ukraine war. Natural gas is widely used for power generation, heating, cooking, and industrial purposes, of which industrial demand accounts for 27-28%. It is mainly used as a raw material in the chemical and fertilizer industries, or used in steel, zinc, aluminum, glass, ceramics, paper, food, and textile sectors that require high-temperature processes around 500 to 1500 °C. It is not something that can be replaced by low-temperature energy from wind and solar power.

In theory, when gas prices rise, companies can respond by cutting production and raising product prices. But in reality, it's not that easy.

First, production cut is easier said than done. Chemical, fertilizer, metal, glass, ceramic, paper, and textile industries, occupying 80% of gas demand, need a highly integrated process in which factories must be in operation 365 days a year including large-scale furnaces or heaters. And approximately 1.5 million people are employed in these industries.

It is not possible to temporarily stop production like weekends off, or reduce production in small units, say 10-20%. It is a matter of whether to shut down a factory or not. Once you stop the operation, it takes 6 months to 1 year in preparation to resume production. According to German statistics, production decreased by 10% in 2022 only. But it does not mean a decrease of production by companies on average, but the cumulative result of the shutdown of unit factories that could not withstand the accumulating losses.

Secondly, it is difficult to pass on rising costs to consumers, too. Most of these products are intermediate goods competing in international markets. Undoubtedly, markets would turn to cheaper Asian and South American products than pricey European products. Fertilizers, for example, is traded in international markets at only half the production costs of Europe.

Steel plants in Bremen and Hamburg have been shut down, a Slovak aluminum producer has laid off two-thirds of its workforce amid record electricity prices, and fertilizer makers in Norway and Germany have halted production and import fertilizer from Latin America. Manufacturers of zinc, sugar, glass, and silicon have shut down their factories. Rumors circulate that BASF's Ludwigshafen plant, which is suffering huge losses, will be completely shut down once the Guangzhou plant in China is built. For the first time since the Industrial Revolution, the EU imports more chemicals than it exports.

If prices rise and delivery is not available, downstream processes bound in the value chain have no choice but to change their suppliers to secure cheap raw materials in a stable manner. They are replaced mostly by imported products and as a result European companies lose their customers. Once companies producing intermediate goods change their supplier, it is not likely the partnership will change for quite a while.

This is just the beginning of what is to come. The EU has set an ambitious target of reducing gas demand by 15%, but they can cut only 1-2% by public campaigns for energy-saving. If the rationing plan is enforced, where will the shock go? The government has no choice but to close factories rather than close schools and hospitals, The education of children and the healthcare of the elderly always take precedence over industrial activities because politicians are reluctant to do things that make voters angry.

Policymakers with a serious look on their face, pledge to come up with energy saving measures and complete the green energy revolution. However, to reach net zero emissions by 2030, renewable energy facilities to produce nearly 30 gigawatts per year are needed, but power generation facilities of only 6.5 gigawatts have been built. Also, among six wind turbines that needs to be installed every day, only one actually built. The gap between the ideal and reality is deepening. Astute conglomerates are curtailing production, shutting down factories, and relocating their business offshore. SMEs with tight cash flow, however, are helpless.

In response to economic downturns, European politicians create hundreds of thousands of public-sector jobs, increase corporate lending and subsidize energy bills. They pledge to invest more in infrastructure, defense, and key industries, and to build a supply chain for electric vehicles, wind power, and solar panel industries. But how, and with what money? Government spending in the Euro Zone already exceeded 50% of GDP. Increased government spending by Western countries amid inflation in the 1970s resulted in stagflation. The same thing is happening in Europe as it was 50 years ago. The ECB, under no bailout clause, will eventually resort to printing money, opening the gate of hell for currency corruption.

3. The Road to China

The United States has taken action to protect its industries by passing the Inflation Reduction Act (IRA), wielding a $ 369 billion incentive package. Strongly criticizing the U.S. scheme, the EU is taking countermeasures. As nationalism has become more prevalent in recent years, protecting domestic industries comes before trade without borders. The WTO system has collapsed de facto.

Corporations that are too large to trade within the borders have to find ways to survive. Amid recent relocation rush to South America and North America, Germany is racing to China. Germany is a major trading country with a trade dependence (ratio of total imports and exports to GDP) reaching 70%, and export dependence is about 40%. China has been Germany's largest trading partner for six consecutive years since 2016, and the trade volume in 2021 is 245 billion euros, which is about 10% of the total trade volume. Of this, 100 billion euros are exports to China.

Volkswagen, the backbone of the German automobile industry, sells 40% of its cars to China. China accounts for around 28% of BMW sales, 22% of Daimler, 13% of Siemens, and 15% of BASF. 46% of German manufacturers import intermediate goods from China. During her 16 years in power, Angela Merkel visited China 12 times, actively pursuing pro-engagement policy towards China. It can safely be said that the economic model that led to Germany's golden age was, simply put, buy cheap Russian energy and export goods to China.

Now that globalization came to an end and the world is being divided into two camps, Germany, which has made its fortune through exports, needs to diversify its business interests in all over the world: Asia, Africa, North America, and South America, etc. There is no doubt that China, the world's largest market for automobile, chemicals, and machinery is still the most attractive investment destinations for individual companies. For German companies, however, political and economic uncertainties in Africa and South America are as high as that in China as they operate their businesses on a large-scale and a long-term basis that take more than 10 years for gestation period of capital. It is a reasonable choice for them to turn to China, a huge market with high growth potential.

For example, BASF's sales to China are around 12 billion euros per annum and the company has been investing 10 billion euro to build a petrochemical complex near Guangzhou. China constitutes 60% of global demand for chemicals and 40% of raw materials. BASF is withdrawing from Europe and investing in China in its desperate effort to survive.

Aldi, Germany's largest discount grocery store chain, plans to open hundreds of stores in China, and Hella, automotive supplier, is striving to double the size of its factory in Shanghai. Siemens has decided to set up a new digital industry division in China, and Volkswagen wants to keep the Urumqi plant running amid the growing international controversy over China's human rights abuses on the Uyghurs in Xinjiang. German industries invested 10 billion euros in China in the first half of 2022 alone. Germany's economic structure consisting of large brand conglomerates and numerous small and medium-sized enterprises (SMEs) leaves no choice but to join hands with China, the world's largest manufacturing power. German industries are now racing towards China at their full speed.

Prime Minister Olaf Scholz acknowledged this reality, and visited Beijing in early November with a gift of allowing Cosco, a state-owned Chinese shipping company, to acquire a 24.99% stake of a container terminal in the Port of Hamburg. On the other hand, Economy Minister Robert Habeck, who came from Green Party in the three-way coalition between SDP, the Greens and the liberal FDP, is particularly hawkish on China and is trying to put a brake on investment in it. Even the coalition government is sharply split over its China policy.

German companies, long plagued by environmentalists' hostilities against their doing business in the country, are at a crucial crossroads to hasten their exit from Europe in the face of the 2022 energy crisis. Now, if they decide to relocate to China, they will face a new hostility from hardliners on China. The German economic model that had brought growth and prosperity to the country for the past 20 years has come to an end. Japan's 'lost two decades' is about to be repeated in Germany.

4. At a Crossroads – Demise or Prosperity

Germany wants to go back to the state before the Russia-Ukraine war. In the event of an armistice, Germany would be willing and able to provide Ukraine with massive reconstruction costs. If Ukraine refuses the offer, Germany could trade with Russia directly by opening the Nord Stream pipelines. But now that Nord Stream has been destroyed, it is not a viable option anymore, and the terms and conditions of the cease-fire can be decided by Ukraine or, more bluntly speaking, by the U.S., Ukraine's biggest ally.

Germany and Russia have been, in fact, industrial allies for the past 20 years. Germany wants Russian energy, and Russia needs German industrial technology. Together, the two countries were able to enjoy prosperity and rise to the European hegemony. The US has long warned against Germany and Russia joining hands, which was clearly highlighted when it opposed the Nord Stream project. Germany is now losing its manufacturing competitiveness as Russia's energy is cut off, and Russia's economy is about to go down due to collective actions by a cartel of oil consuming countries. And the next target to be placed under the U.S. measures will be the economic alliance between Germany and China.

Germany, complacent with its past 20 years of prosperity, has unfortunately failed to develop industries to replace manufacturing. Deutsche Bank pulled out of global equity sales and trading, and Commerzbank has long diminished into domestic banks. Switzerland's UBS, which can be seen as a pan-German capital (Switzerland's first official language is German), withdrew from Wall Street in 2008, and Credit Suisse was unable to overcome the shock of the meltdown of Archegos Capital Management and took the Saudi royal family as one of the biggest shareholders.

Germany has long given up electronics, semiconductor, and computer industries, and has no big-tech companies even with the huge single market called the EU. The failure of Wirecard, a fintech payment company whose market cap once surpassed Deutsche Bank's and the fall of Greensill Capital of the UK, raised a deep skepticism about whether European big-tech companies are really possible.

What will be the future of Europe, whose manufacturing has been hollowed out and which has also failed to develop electronics, finance, and tech industries? In particular, what will be the future of Germany's economy, which has reigned as Europe's manufacturing powerhouse in reliance on manufacturing for a quarter of its employment? If the

European industry is hollowed out, will it finally open a door of opportunity for Korean companies that have been struggling in the European market?

Europe is likely to return to a stronger protectionism. More protectionist measures will be introduced to help regional companies, such as strengthening carbon credits and ESG regulations, providing hundreds of billions of euros in energy subsidies to regional companies, and introducing a carbon tax tantamount to border tariffs. After all, the European market belongs to Europeans, and other countries in the region will emerge to replace Germany.

Then, what countries are potential candidates? It should be the ones with a sufficient consumer market and low-wage labor force, simple environmental regulations, and suitable marine transportation. Poland and Turkey are the only places in Europe that meet these conditions. The year 2022 would be marked in the history of world economy as the beginning of Europe's descent into deindustrialization. And my humble prediction is that the era of Germany be over and Poland and Turkey wake up from their long slumber to a future in which they emerge as Europe's industrial leaders.

High Oil Prices and Weak Yen Cast Shadow[1)]

1. Two Variables

Oil prices recently surpassed $90 per barrel. It can be attributed to the production cuts of 1 million barrels per day by Saudi Arabia and 300,000 barrels by Russia, the world's top two oil exporters. Both have expressed their intent to maintain production reductions as a precautionary measure against demand shortages.

The dollar-to-yen exchange rate is also nearing 150 yen. Despite the widening interest rate gap between the U.S. and Japan, the Bank of Japan is not raising interest rates to address more than two decades of deflation. Wall Street investment banks caution that the exchange rate could potentially reach as high as 160 to 170 yen.

Oil prices and exchange rates are critical external variables shaping the Korean economy. Korea achieved robust growth in the 1980s thanks to what is often referred

---

1) This column was published on September 15, 2023.

to as the 'three lows': low oil prices, low interest rates, and the low exchange rate (or a strong yen, in other words). Among these factors, interest rates currently pose a lesser concern due to the improved resilience of corporate financial structures following the Korean financial crisis. High interest rates do exert significant pressure on household debt and project finance but primarily affect the domestic asset market, which is unrelated to the international competitiveness of Korean companies.

Although South Korea is far distant from major oil-producing regions, high oil prices place a significant burden on the cost structure of Korean companies. Additionally, a weaker yen could lead to renewed competition with Japanese companies, which we may have forgotten for some time. Now, if we find ourselves in a situation opposite to that of the 1980s, with high oil prices, high interest rates, and a depreciated yen, can South Korea weather these challenges? How long will high oil prices and the weak yen persist?

2. Crisis that can be Brought by High Oil Prices

1) War in Ukraine without a Mediator

Undoubtedly, the primary reason for the high oil prices is the war in Ukraine. Russia is the world's second-largest oil exporter, producing 10 million barrels and exporting 6 million barrels to the global market per day. Russia and Ukraine both claim to be winning the war, but the reality of the conflict, which has been ongoing for over a year and a half, is a grueling war of attrition. To bring an end to the war, intervention from a third party is necessary.

Ukraine is already preparing for a major offensive next spring, while Russia is reaching out to North Korea to bolster its armory. It now appears certain that the war will last for more than three years, in contrast to the optimistic predictions made at the beginning of the year, which suggested it would not extend beyond the end of this year. Is there no ceasefire or mediator in sight?

EU nations naturally did not want the conflict to continue, as they were facing economic hardship due to the disruption of Russian oil supplies following the war in their vicinity. At the onset of the war, French President

Emmanuel Macron traveled to Russia in an attempt to mediate, while Silvio Berlusconi, the former Italian prime minister who passed away in June of this year, also expressed his willingness to mediate, highlighting his friendship with Putin. France has traditionally maintained pro-Russian sentiments, and Italy, as an energy ally, has been importing Russian oil since 1959. Nevertheless, the protracted war has led to unforeseen political and economic consequences, prompting EU nations to alter their approach.

Germany is the EU's largest stakeholder, and it wouldn't be an exaggeration to state that Germany holds significant influence over EU policy-making. With the backing of fiscally conservative Northern European countries and the pan-Germanic economies of Central and Eastern Europe, Germany has wielded substantial control within the EU. Its sound government finances and the strength of German companies have been key factors driving its leadership role in the European Union.

However, as energy cutoff inflicts damage on German manufacturing and prompts a corporate exodus, each country is now recalculating its priorities. In 2022 alone, foreign direct investment (FDI) from German businesses amounted to €135 billion, with a substantial 70% of that directed towards EU member states. German companies are now traversing the European continent like nomads in search of affordable and reliable sources of energy. The relocation of energy-dependent German firms to other EU countries is akin to a welcomed rain in times of drought for these nations. It brings benefits such as increased employment opportunities, greater investments, and improved growth rates. Importantly, this trend is expected to endure as long as these German companies exist.

As if reflecting this, the German economy is clearly experiencing a recession, while most other EU countries have returned to positive growth. The protracted war has eroded Germany's standing in Europe, while strengthening the positions of other nations. France and Italy, unexpectedly benefiting, are reconsidering their stance on the prolonged war. The U.S. and U.K. show no intention of intervening, and France and Italy have shifted from their initial anti-war stance to a state of silence. The war in Ukraine has lost its mediators.

2) Objectives of Saudi Arabia and Russia

Some suggest that the oil production cuts are a preemptive measure to brace for a potential decrease in demand amid a global economic downturn and to compensate for budget shortfalls in both Saudi Arabia and Russia. They argue that Saudi Crown Prince Salman requires substantial funds for the construction of Neom City and for implementing extensive reform initiatives, and Russia also faces significant expenses in the war in Ukraine.

However, the global energy industry is not that simple. When Saudi Arabia, which exports 8 million barrels per day, and Russia, which exports 6 million barrels per day, reduce their production by 1 million barrels and 300,000 barrels, respectively, it translates to losing 12.5% and 5% of their customer base. Those countries that are no longer able to secure oil from Saudi Arabia and Russia will need to seek out new suppliers, but since oil trade involves international agreements, re-establishing lost trade relationships is not an easy process. Venezuela struggled to find buyers in the international oil market in the 1960s, and Qatar, which developed the massive North Field gas field in the Persian Gulf, spent some time wandering the global gas market looking for natural gas buyers.

Historically, OPEC's discussions and implementation of production cuts have not always proceeded smoothly.

Second, high oil prices don't last for a long time. High oil prices enable the development of costly fields. Shale wells, which have production costs of around $57 per barrel, become attractive for large-scale investment because they are expected to generate consistent profits. Even fields in extremely cold regions with production costs exceeding $70 per barrel can become profitable under these conditions. Moreover, elevated oil prices often incentivize the growth of alternative energy industries, such as solar and wind power.

Lastly, high oil prices can come back to haunt oil-producing nations as oil-consuming countries may reduce their oil consumption during economic recessions triggered by these prices. The value for oil exports is calculated from the exported volume multiplied by the export price, and if price growth outpaces volume decline, it leads to a decrease in the overall value of oil exports. Zak Yamani, Saudi Arabia's oil minister, opposed OPEC's decision to decrease oil production during the 1973 Yom Kippur War, arguing that it would ultimately harm oil-producing nations.

Why are Saudi Arabia and Russia cutting oil production, even though it appears to be detrimental to their economies? To influence the 2024 U.S. presidential election.

3) Outlook for the Oil Market in 2024

Saudi Crown Prince bin Salman is considered a reformist monarch who broke the Saudi royal tradition of inheriting the throne set by the founder, King Ibn Saud. He has seized assets belonging to the royalty and cracked down on the media to suppress domestic discontent. Additionally, he is suspected of involvement in the murder of Washington Post journalist Jamal Khashoggi. Since taking office, President Biden has consistently called for democratization in Saudi Arabia and has pledged to isolate the kingdom on the international stage.

Russia also requires an exit strategy to quell the growing public discontent stemming from the prolonged war and to bring an end to the conflict. The Russian populace has grown weary of the war, as indicated by the Wagner Group rebellion, and it's nearly impossible to envision Russia's weakened military sustaining the conflict for more than a year and a half. However, with no mediator in the picture, Putin finds himself without a viable means to conclude the war.

If there is a shared interest between both countries, it would be preventing Biden's re-election. In the event that oil prices surge, leading to inflation and hardship for American citizens, it could jeopardize Biden's chances of being re-elected. This scenario draws parallels to the re-election loss of former President Jimmy Carter (who served from 1977 to 1981), where high oil prices and interest rates eroded his support. If Trump were to make another bid for the presidency, Saudi Arabia could potentially work towards normalizing relations with the United States, a crucial component of Saudi Arabia's security, and legitimize Crown Prince bin Salman as the heir to the throne. In a similar vein, Putin might explore the possibility of a ceasefire with Trump acting as a mediator.

However, it seems unlikely that deliberate cuts by both countries will deter Biden. The U.S. administration possesses a range of tools to address this situation. To begin with, it could consider imposing windfall profit taxes on oil companies. Italy's Prime Minister Meloni has shown that this approach is possible in Western countries by levying windfall taxes on financial firms that benefited from rising interest rates.

A more fundamental means would be to decouple domestic prices from international oil prices. The Single Price System, which has been in place since Russia's reentry into the global oil market in 1990, is not that old. Oil prices were first determined by Standard Oil, then by the Texas Railroad Commission during World War I and II. After World War II, they were set by the major oil companies, often referred to as the Seven Sisters, and after 1973, by OPEC. Since the mid-1980s, as oil from non-OPEC regions flooded international markets, driven by high prices, oil prices have largely been set by financial markets in New York and London.

Following the conflict in Ukraine, the single price system was divided into two prices: the international price and the Russian price. There is also the potential for the introduction of a "US domestic price" as a third pricing system. The U.S., a market economy, has a history of frequent market interventions in oil, including price controls, import quotas, and fueling order. A third price tag would not be out of the ordinary.

This can also benefit the shale oil industry. The oncestable shale sector faced significant losses during the pandemic when oil prices sharply declined. Wall Street investors had flocked to shale stocks with expectations of consistent dividend income like bonds, but the industry's high-cost structure couldn't endure the low oil prices during the pandemic, leading to bankruptcies and acquisitions. Now that oil prices have recovered, Wall Street investors are demanding immediate dividends and increases in stock prices from shale operators, rather than business expansion.

If a third pricing system is introduced and U.S. domestic oil prices stabilize within the range of $60 to $70, shale businesses could avoid the risk associated with low oil prices and become a new alternative for investors. Shale oil fields, that cost around $8 million per well, can generate steady cash flows, rendering them a long-term investment option akin to U.S. Treasuries and commercial real estate. There is no reason why Wall Street shouldn't welcome this new pricing scheme.

4) Threat of High Oil Prices to the South Korean Economy

South Korea possesses one of the world's most energy-dependent economic models. While its economy accounts for 1.6% of the global economy, the country is a large oil consumer responsible for approximately 2.9 million barrels per day, or 3% of global oil consumption. The driver behind this high oil consumption is apparently its flagship industries such as heavy chemical industries, automobiles, steel production, shipbuilding, machinery, and petrochemicals.

China and Japan, both of which employ similar economic models with Korea and are competitors, also import oil, but China does not buy oil at international prices. China produces about one-third of its oil domestically, while the remaining two-thirds are acquired through long-term contracts with oil-producing countries based on its substantial demand, and, importantly, the country can access Russian and Iranian oil which tends to be more affordable compared to global oil prices. It is certain that China's average oil import prices are lower than those of Korea.

Japan, with a population of 120 million, consumes only 3.4 million barrels of oil per day. Despite having a similar economic model to Korea, Japan's lower oil consumption can be attributed to the fact that its manufacturing sector produces 25% of its output overseas. Assuming the Korean economy consumes 1.05 billion barrels of oil per year and purchases 50% of it at international prices on the spot market, a $10 increase in oil prices would result in an additional cost of $5.25 billion per year. If the price were to increase from $70 to $100 per barrel, the outflow of foreign currency would increase by more than $15 billion.

Higher oil prices create a cost disadvantage for China, and Japan and South Korea face a similar competitive disadvantage. However, Japan has a secret weapon that has boosted its economy recently: a weak yen. Now, let's examine the significant impact that the yen weakness will have on the Korean economy.

3. Crisis that can be Brought by the Weak Yen

1) The Germany of Asia, Japan

Germany's reliance on the U.S. for security, Russia for energy, and China for market has faced criticism for being unsustainable. There is a country in Asia that does the same: Japan.

When President Nixon announced the Nixon Doctrine in Guam in December 1969 encouraging Asian nations to handle the problems of international security themselves, the Japanese government was taken by surprise. Sensing the emerging détente, Prime Minister Kakuei Tanaka visited China in September 1972 and Japan made a swift decision to establish diplomatic relations with China seven years before the United States. Deng Xiaoping, upon assuming power in 1978, made Japan his first diplomatic stop and expressed eagerness to attract investments from Japanese companies.

Japanese investment in China began in the 1990s to leverage China's cost-effective labor force, particularly in less prominent industries. After China's accession to the WTO in 2001, larger Japanese corporations also entered the market. As of June 2022, Japan stands as the second-largest investor in China, and the number of Japanese companies operating in China was 12,706. Japanese conglomerates operate across various industries in China, including automotive, electronics, chemicals, textiles, and machinery.

For instance, Toyota Motor Corporation sells 2 million vehicles annually in China, and Honda and Nissan sell around 1.5 million vehicles. Leading electronics companies like Matsushita Electric, Toshiba, NEC, Hitachi, and Fujitsu operate their own factories and local research institutes in China, and textile and chemical firms such as Asahi Kasei, Mitsubishi Chemical, and Mitsui Chemicals, along with heavy equipment manufacturers like Komatsu and Hitachi Construction Machinery that are seeking business opportunities tied to the Belt and Road Initiative, cannot leave China. Twenty-five percent of Japan's manufacturing activities take place overseas, and of that, around 30 percent is done in China. A Japanese politician, speaking on condition of anonymity, says that "Decoupling from China is unthinkable."

Japan is also looking to partner with Russia in the energy sector. The plan involves importing natural gas from East Siberia as part of its transition towards a low-carbon economy. This project is known as Power of Siberia 1 and 2. Although the war in Ukraine has temporarily slowed down the project, Japan anticipates a future supply of affordable gas through the East Siberian pipeline, which will signal a revival of Japanese manufacturing.

Japan has energy ties with Russia and is unable to leave the Chinese market, but some officials blame Putin for the war in Ukraine and voice readiness to wage war if China attacks Taiwan. What alternatives does Japan have?

2) Weaker yen, Reverse Plaza Agreement, and Reshoring

My column titled "Concerns in the Superdollar Era" published on September 26, 2022, discusses the idea that the yen depreciation, which began last summer, might not be solely due to the U.S.-Japan interest rate differential, but possibly a result of what could be called a "reverse Plaza Agreement". Japanese companies are reporting record-high profits, and the Nikkei stock index is soaring. After remaining stagnant for three decades, wages and prices are now showing signs of increasing. But is there more to the story?

The Japanese government has allocated around ¥2 trillion annually and pledged subsidies to incentivize Japanese companies to reshore during Trump's anti-China campaign. Nevertheless, no matter how substantial these subsidies are, companies will not relocate their factories unless it is economically viable. Japan is perceived as an expensive country for manufacturers due to its high labor costs, labor shortages, costly electricity, exorbitant land prices, and a range of other factors.

However, should the dollar reach a rate of 160 to 170 yen, things would change. If the yen were to depreciate by approximately 50 percent from around 110 yen, executives at companies like the Toyota Motor Corporation and Matsushita Electric would need to carefully consider their options. With the assurance of a consistently weaker yen, they might contemplate relocating operations back to Japan instead of establishing new factories in China amid escalating geopolitical tensions. Neither Trump, Biden, Abe, nor Kishida will mandate Japanese companies to reshore, but they may voluntarily opt for it, driven by the substantial advantages offered by a weaker yen. This is how a democratic economy operates.

The outcome would likely entail a weakened Chinese economy and a revitalized Japanese economy. American, Japanese, Korean, and eventually German companies might exit the Chinese market. Where will the Chinese economy source its vitality if these four manufacturing giants are unwilling to invest? Japan could resemble the United States in 2023: with new factories, increased employment, robust domestic demand, and a revitalized economy.

Interestingly, Kazuo Ueda, the Governor of the Bank of Japan, was invited to the FRB's Jackson Hole meeting in August 2023. Why did Governor Ueda go to Jackson Hole? Perhaps they were there to enjoy the refreshing air of this vacation spot, to reflect on the achievements of the U.S. and Japanese central banks, and to reaffirm their commitment to working together in the international foreign exchange market.

4. Conclusion – In 2024, South Korean Companies are Expected to Begin Losing Competitiveness

High oil prices elevate costs, eroding price competitiveness of South Korean companies. They also trigger recessions and dampen global demand. If oil prices indeed reach $100 to $120 per barrel next year, as anticipated by oil market experts, it's evident that the export-dependent South Korean economy will face hardships.

Nevertheless, it's unlikely that high oil prices can be sustained for more than a few years. Non-OPEC countries account for 60 percent of global oil production, and new shale fields will start production. Furthermore, it's reassuring to note that the competitors in the global market, Korea, China, and Japan, are facing similar circumstances, though to varying extents.

The weak yen is a completely different matter, though. It implies that formidable Japanese electronics and automotive companies, which we've somewhat overlooked for a while, are coming back to the global stage. Can Korean electronics and automotive companies withstand the challenge posed by over a dozen prominent Japanese counterparts armed with the weak yen?

In the 1980s, Japanese electronics companies dominated the world market, defeating American and European competitors one after another. In the automotive sector, the United States relinquished its title of the automotive powerhouse to Japan long ago. GM and Ford have essentially become regional players, focusing mainly on light truck production under protectionist policies in North America.

After four decades of eager anticipation, the U.S. electronics and automotive industries are now ready. Apple's iPhone has thrown the Japanese electronics sector into turmoil, and Tesla has disrupted the premium car market traditionally dominated by Germany and Japan. In short, the U.S. is poised to counter any potential Japanese advances in the electronics and automotive industries.

What weapons can Korean companies carry to the global market where the U.S. leverages innovation and Japan benefits from the exchange rate? Korean companies, which need to mainly target the Western world in a global market divided into the West and non-West, struggle to match the same level of innovative content as U.S. companies and are no match for Japan, which is armed with the weak yen. This is why it is concerning to envision the future implications of the weak yen. It is now more crucial than ever for the government to respond promptly.

Watching out for the Resurgence of Japan's Electronics Industry (Part I)[1]

1. The Weak Yen and What It Means

An economy is the sum of a variety of industrial activities. The primary industry consists of agriculture, fisheries, and livestock, the secondary industry includes mining and manufacturing, and the tertiary industry is mostly in the services sector. The tertiary industry encompasses a wide range of businesses from food & beverage, hospitality, tourism, finance, education, healthcare, media to engineering services with Big Tech companies included as well.

In the secondary industry, the share of the manufacturing sector differs widely in developed countries. Manufacturing takes up as much as 25% of Korea and Germany's economy and more than 20% of Japan's GDP. It accounts for around 10% of the total output in the United States, but only single

---

1) This column was published on February 6, 2024.

digits in most European countries. The decline is largely linked to the "hollowing out". On the other hand, China, dubbed as the world's factory has the manufacturing percentage share about 30% of its GDP.

GDP is defined as the sum of the money value of the production of all three sectors -primary, secondary, and tertiary industries. The total value added by a firm is basically equal to the sum of labor costs, expenses, and profits excluding cost of raw materials. The lower the raw material cost, the more value added in the industry. Steel and chemical industries have a material cost ratio of up to 70-80%, while automobiles, shipbuilding, and machinery are of about 40%. The electronics industry, in the meantime, has a wide range of spectrum from white goods that require high raw material costs to semiconductors and computers that are high value-added products. The service sector, generally known as a tertiary industry usually requires so little material cost that their production is mostly value added. It is the reason behind the high involvement of developed countries in tertiary sector.

Korea, China, Japan, and Germany which have higher share of the secondary sector need to add value in such industries to cultivate strong economic growth and per capita income. Japan's strong automobile and consumer electronics business helped it rise to the world's second largest economy in the 80's and Korea had escaped the middle-income trap following a similar economic model.

China's nominal GDP is $18.5 trillion, and per capita income is about $13,000. Its main industries remain in steel, chemicals, automobiles, shipbuilding, and machinery, and these smokestack businesses do not produce very high value added. However, if China grows out of the US-Japan's subcontract assembly factories for consumer electronics and creates new products with higher added value, its per capita income could easily go over $20,000. In that case, China may be poised to eclipse the US as the world's biggest economy since the US nominal GDP is around $28 trillion and Chinese population of 1.4 billion x $20,000 is $28 trillion. This is the basis for some analysts forecasting China's surge to global economic dominance. Everyone knows that China is struggling with its real estate crisis, but as a matter of fact, the future of the Chinese economy is largely hinged on the development of the consumer electronics industry.

The United States has been keeping close tabs on China's semiconductor industry, but it will not be able to block global demand for Chinese consumer electronic products. Apple iPhone is a good example. To keep China's consumer electronics industry at bay, meticulous precautionary measures are needed. The US and Japan have declared a full-scale cooperation and weak yen is their first step.

2. The Rise and Fall of the US Consumer Electronics Industry

It is said that the Second Industrial Revolution, also known as the Technological Revolution in the electrical and electronic industries started in the United States and was completed in Japan. At the core of the industrial revolution were telephones, radios, and televisions, and AT&T and RCA, two most powerful companies in the United States, dominated the industries.

It was RCA that dominated the consumer electronics industry. It beat out the rival CBS and finally came to conquer markets worldwide by inventing the 'tricolor picture tube' that was compatible with existing black-and-white TVs. RCA formed NBC to take control of broadcasting, and it became the world's largest producer of consumer electronics by the 1960s with soaring revenue from radio and TV sales, technology transfer and broadcasting rights.

In the meanwhile, the budding semiconductor industry was growing under the auspices of the US Department of Defense. After two world wars, the United States overtook Great Britain to become the leader of the "free world", but the world it inherited was a dangerous one. Western allies were in ruins or weakened, and enemies across the Atlantic and Pacific Ocean - Soviet Union and Communist China - were far more populous and callous to civilian casualties. With its smaller population, the only way for the United States to stand against these countries was to increase the precision and destructive power of its weapons.

AT&T and RCA were at the forefront of the early semiconductor industry. AT&T Bell Labs and RCA's Sarnoff Labs were private research labs specializing in communications and TV technology, but they were able to conduct creative research like university labs, funded by companies with enormous profits in virtual monopolies. The Department of Defense also sponsored them to develop new semiconductor technologies.

Afterwards, these companies' unrivaled technological prowess and market position were put under antitrust scrutiny. In 1958 the Department of Justice forced RCA, AT&T, and IBM to provide its patent portfolio to US competitors at no cost. Although RCA's technologies were made public, US companies focused on making and selling replica parts rather than developing new and better TVs. RCA wound up licensing its technology to European and Japanese companies, complacent in pocketing hefty royalties. In the meantime, more Japanese companies were growing at a dazzling speed.

To deal with the monopoly issues, RCA adopted a strategy of diversifying into the production of largely unrelated product lines. Inspired by IBM's success, it entered the mainframe computer business and set on an aggressive acquisition course taking over companies in the food, rental cars, and carpet manufacturing in an attempt to build a multinational conglomerate. However, enormous financial losses in the mainframe computer business and a series of acquisitions depleted RCA's funds and ultimately caused the downfall of the once dominant tech company in the face of increasing challenges from Japanese firms. After several failed attempts, it aborted its Video Cassette

Recorder project.

The 1958 Consent Decree of the Justice Department to make patents available to interested parties failed to grow new companies, and the collapse of RCA resulted in the fall of the entire U.S. consumer electronics industry. If RCA had stayed focused on its original business areas instead of diversifying its product lines, it could be still enjoying a dominant position in the consumer electronics market. RCA made a series of major strategic mistakes and it brought down the whole American consumer electronics industry.

The revolutionary technologies developed by Bell Labs and Sarnoff Labs, however, did not go unnoticed. Those across the sea were paying close attention to the technologies - the Japanese.

3. Japan's Global Dominance: Imitation and Creation (I)

In the 1960s, tech firms, influenced by American firms, started mushrooming in Japan. They grew by imitating their American rivals, the Big Four of the electronics and computer industry - AT&T, RCA, IBM and XEROX. Japanese companies like Matsushita, Sanyo, Toshiba and Hitachi followed the typical growth path of large firms by imitating American technology and marketing. In the fierce format war for video cassette recorder standard, for instance, Matsushita and its sister company Sanyo won the global standard against Sony and Philips with outstanding maneuvering skills in marketing and distribution channels.

At the same time, there were many creative entrepreneurs in Japan. In the 1960s, they made semiconductors commercially viable, which had been invented by AT&T and RCA and used for military purposes. They include Canon, Casio, Seiko, and Yamaha with Sony and Sharp in front. The two major players have grown into large companies producing a full lineup of products. These two firms were teeming with creative entrepreneurs and inventors, ready to take risks and quick to make moves. Now let's have a close look at how they came to dominate the world of consumer electronics.

1) CMOS Chip: Crystal Wristwatch and Calculator

Throughout the 1960s, Bulova of the United States led the watchmaking industry. Bulova Accutron used an electrically powered tuning fork having the error less than one minute per month, which was an unprecedented precision level compared to mechanical watches at the time. However, a more innovative technology had already been out there.

In 1922, RCA engineer Walter Cady discovered that a quartz crystal under oscillating currents resonates at very precise and more stable frequencies. The only problem was excessive battery consumption, and it had to be dealt with by creating CMOS chip that consumes less power.

There were times when watches "made in Japan" were seen as "cheapie". A wristwatch that showed Arabic numerals on a fluorescent display was no comparison to the Swiss Made label, famed for its quality and craftsmanship. Watches are not simply a device that tells the time, but serve as status symbols, often being a key indicator of a person's wealth and taste.

Seiko had thought that developing a CMOS chip would take them many years of development by dozens of researchers. Then Jean Hoerni from RCA came to rescue.

When Hoerni came up with the idea of using CMOS ICs in watches, he went first to Swiss watchmakers to fund his research, but was turned down by the artisan-turned-managers who had no idea about semiconductors. In dismay, he flew to Japan where he met Chairman of Seiko, and inked the deal. Seiko was able to ship its first batch of CMOS chips in November 1971.

Seiko's quartz timepiece was a hit and turned the watch industry upside down in a dramatic way. It was much more accurate than existing electronic watches and had attractive design, and above all, came with a more affordable price tag. In 1974 Seiko licensed its patents to other Japanese companies, enabling Japanese watchmakers to emerge as a global leader in the watch industry. Thanks to cheap quartz wristwatches, global demand for watches doubled in the late 1970s, and in the meanwhile Swiss watchmakers with hundreds of years of handicraft manufacturing went downhill.

―――――○――――――――○―――――

Until the 1960s, calculators were typewriter-sized and had a visual output on vacuum tube fluorescent display. Back then, it was much cheaper and faster to employ an accountant who could use the Chinese abacus skillfully rather than buying cumbersome and expensive calculators.

In the early 1970s, the calculator war broke out in the desktop calculator market. More than 60 companies jumped into the calculator market. But in order to commercialize the calculators, they needed to develop CMOS chips and display technology with lower power consumption.

Sharp, a pioneer in display industry, began mass production of a liquid crystal display (LCD) that was as energy-efficient as CMOS chips by applying a vacuum tube fluorescent display. It also developed small photovoltaic cells to be mounted on the device, paving the way for solar-powered desktop calculators that did not even require batteries. The driving force behind those accomplishments by Sharp was Tadashi Sasaki, also known as 'Rocket Sasaki', a legendary Japanese engineer.

When the cut-throat war of pocket calculators was over, only four survived - Japan's Sharp and Casio, and America's Texas Instruments and Hewlett Packard. In 1980 alone, about 120 million units were produced, and Japanese companies accounted for half of them.

Quartz wristwatches and calculator chips were the first mass-produced CMOS products. Seiko Epson, born after the merge in 1985, supplied CMOS chips to fabless companies including Xilinx, Lattice Semiconductor, and Cirrus Logic in the United States. Sharp established a foundry partnership with Altera, a Xilinx competitor. Intel invented the world's first DRAM using the CMOS chip. CMOS chips became a big cash cow for Seiko and Sharp.

2) LCD: Seiko and Sharp

In May 1968, RCA unveiled the first liquid crystal display TV. They claimed that the TVs of tomorrow would be as thin as a notebook, free of bulky cathode ray tubes. However, the engineering hurdles associated with scaling up their prototypes to a full-size liquid crystal TV set remained high, and senior management was gradually losing faith in this "linear model" and its commercialization. In the end, RCA's LCD research group was left in shambles.

Sharp paid RCA about $3 million in licensing LCD. After making a profit by selling calculators in the 1970s, Sharp invested a staggering $200 million in LCD. In the history of science, there were cases that the same research took place concurrently in completely different places, and LCD technology was one of them. Seiko developed independently the thin, spiral LCD based on the technology licensed from Hoffmann-La Roche of Switzerland. While Sharp wanted to utilize the LCD technology in making calculators, Seiko's goal was to make a TV watch with a built-in LCD screen.

Shinji Morozumi of Seiko held a press conference in Tokyo in May 1983 to demonstrate its full-color pocket LCD television, which was what RCA had envisioned 15 years ago. Seiko finally brought the world's first commercially available portable color television My Channel to the market in 1984. Seiko's portable LCD TVs took other big Japanese companies like Matsushita, Toshiba, and Hitachi by surprise, and they jumped into the market with both feet.

Seiko, having no distribution network, needed another breakthrough to commercialize its LCD technology. Most of all, prices of the products had to be lowered by means of mass production. In other words, LCD must be used as a component.

The first product using LCDs is a light valve used in office beam projectors. Then Seiko went on to adopt the LCD technology in electronic viewfinders of the video camera. Seiko's dominance in the market remained unchallenged until Sony and other video camera manufacturers developed their own LCD viewfinders. The third product using the technology was an image reader in the facsimile machines. It works in the way that the facsimile scanner examines whatever document you feed into it and converts its image into an electric signal.

In 1985 Seiko merged with Epson an electronic printer company to establish Seiko-Epson Corporation. Seiko-Epson took full advantage of Epson's share in the office supplies market and Seiko's LCD technology to become a global leader in the office electronics market.

―――――○―――――○―――――

Sharp launched the first electronic calculator to use an LCD in April 1973, and finally succeeded in mass producing EL (electroluminescence) flat panel displays in 1983. With amazing creativity, Tadashi Sasaki at Sharp made possible what everyone was skeptical about, saying that it was impossible to incorporate thin film transistors to LCDs. In the same year, NASA announced that it would apply Sharp's display methods for the space shuttle's navigation system. The world was again amazed at Sharp's technological prowess.

Sharp's mass production of new LCD application products helped it take up around 40% of the global LCD market in the mid-1990s. Sharp viewcam camcorders with LCD screen, handheld LCD touch screen terminals, and digital still cameras were huge hits in the 1990s. Best of all, they pioneered the new laptop computer market.

Unfortunately, Sharp that was the global leader of the consumer electronics market along with Sony until the mid-1990s, is now gone. Sharp rose to the dominant player in the global electronics industry thanks to the LCD technology, but it was also the LCD that led to Sharp's demise. In the mid-2000s, it made large-scale investments in LCD facilities, but fell into an irrecoverable state after huge losses in the wake of the sudden appreciation of the yen. Sharp, known for innovative and pioneering ideas led by 'Rocket Sasaki', was taken over by Taiwanese manufacturer Foxconn in 2016, putting an end to its saga.

3) CCD: Sony's Challenge

AT&T's long-time goal was to develop Picturephone. When researchers at Bell Labs finally invented the CCD image capture device and introduced the world's first black-and-white analogue videophone in 1971, the market response to the new product was surprisingly bad.

A charge-coupled device (CCD) is a kind of a "semiconductor eye" that consumes less power and works well even in low light environments. It was useful for night reconnaissance and suited for military purposes including cruise missiles. However, for commercial use, reducing costs in mass production and colorization were crucial. Bell Labs engineers turned to the Navy for R&D funds, but the Navy turned down saying the black and white CCDs were good enough, and AT&T executives had no intention of further investment, having already spent $500 million on the development of the Picturephone.

On the contrary, Sony's third president Kazuo Iwama decided to bet his luck on the development of color CCD imaging systems in 1973. For over 10 years, he pushed forward against enormous cost and massive opposition within the company. Just as it had developed the transistor and created a completely new type of radio, Sony invested in CCD to create a completely new type of camera.

Fighting a seemingly losing battle "with swords broken and arrows run out" for years, Sony finally succeeded in developing a practical level CCD camera in March 1978, five years after the onset of the project. And in early 1982, Sony completed the world's first CCD semiconductor assembly line in 10 years.

Sony released the first video camcorder employing CCD in January 1985. Sony CCD-V8 was capable of recording video on standard 8mm videotape. What began from heavy, shoulder-bearing cameras has evolved into what could be held in hands. After a full year of Sony's monopoly, Matsushita-owned JVC released VHS-C camcorder, and Sharp also entered the CCD market. Since then, the three big Japanese companies have long maintained a virtual oligopoly in the CCD and camcorder markets.

CCDs formed the basis of the early digital still cameras in the mid-1990s and helped Sony to rise to the world's largest camera manufacturer. A complete victory of the Japanese consumer electronics over the German optical industry. Now camcorders and digital cameras are integrated into and replaced by smartphones, but Sony still makes more than half of the global image sensors used in smartphones.

4) Semiconductor Laser: Optical Communication, Personal Copier, CD Player

Morton Panish and Izuo Hayashi of Bell Labs played a key role in designing the first semiconductor laser that operate continuously at room temperature in 1970. Along with the breakthrough made by Corning scientists in the same year - the glass fibers with low signal loss, the semiconductor laser showed the potential to make optical communication feasible.

It took years, however, Bell Labs to push forward with the optical communications technology. This was because its parent company, AT&T, had invested too much of its money on the millimeter waveguide communication system. Kaneyuki Kurokawa of Bell Labs, one of the most vocal critics of the millimeter waveguides, was convinced of the potential of the semiconductor laser in optical communication system. When the world's first testbed for optical communications was successfully demonstrated, he tried to talk AT&T management into supporting his research and development. But disheartened by the hesitant management, Kaneyuki headed directly to Japan in 1977, where he joined Fujitsu. Izuo Hayashi, too, joined NEC's Research Labs much earlier in 1971. The race to capitalize on semiconductor lasers has begun among large Japanese companies.

The year 1983 was one of the most shameful years in AT&T history. AT&T was awarded a $250 million contract to design a major portion of the first trans-Atlantic fiber optic submarine cable called TAT-8, but AT&T did not have capabilities to implement the project. It turned to Japan's Hitachi for help. And the next year Hitachi Research Institute developed a semiconductor laser that could operate successfully for over 1 million hours.

Canon has come a long way since its days as a manufacturer of cheap cameras with an aim to beat Leica the German camera maker, and it went on to make copiers since 1970. Canon executives were excited to see the long-life semiconductor laser developed by Hitachi. The semiconductor lasers were small in size and required very low operating energy, and their price was as affordable as other semiconductors. Canon decided to go for personal copiers.

The world's first personal copying machines were released in 1982. Hewlett-Packard printer division were fascinated by Canon's prototype and signed on a joint business deal with Canon. Canon was in charge of supplying HP with laser printer engines and manufacturing printers and HP developing software that would run the printer. Xerox "dry" photocopiers, large enough to fill a room, were replaced by ones as small as the size of a refrigerator.

Canon created an entirely new market for personal use copiers, and Xerox was left in bitter defeat. Xerox was so used to dealing with large corporate customers that it did not capture new opportunities, having no idea about the market demands for personal printers for small businesses. Now laser jet printers have become small enough to fit on a desk.

Robert Hall of GE R&D Labs made gallium arsenide tunnel diodes that oscillated at a frequency of up to 5 billion revolutions per second. He wanted to convince the

U.S. Department of Defense that the new light-emitting diodes (LEDs) would be a new star in optical wireless communication technology. It made possible to send a TV signal by LED light from a mountain 30 miles away, but it had clear limitations. The system did not work in rainy or cloudy weather, making it useless on the battlefields.

GE researchers applied for a patent on the technology at the end of 1962 and finally obtained the patent in 1966, but no one could come up with product applications of the laser diode. Sony and Philips, the Dutch tech company, rushed for an opportunity.

Sony, having lost the war for the video cassette recorder standard, was desperate to develop a new product and formed a business partnership with Philips. Heitaro Nakajima who was a pioneer in digital audio, was leading Sony's Compact Disc project. And at last, in October 1982, Sony launched the portable CD player 'Discman', following the Walkman. With the advent of CD players, major companies such as Hitachi, Matsushita, Mitsubishi Electric, NEC, Toshiba, and Sharp rushed in, driving the new CD player market to take off.

4. Concluding Summary of Part I

Bell Labs not only invented the transistor, but also contributed to the fundamental development in semiconductor technology and semiconductor laser technology, and later created CCD cameras. RCA played a major role in establishing the early technological base of CMOS technology, LCDs, thin film transistor and solar cell technology.

These innovative inventions have paved the way for portable calculators, quartz wristwatches, LCD TVs, camcorders, digital cameras, optical communications, personal copiers, and CD players. It is tragic that the US consumer electronics industry failed to tap on these groundbreaking inventions that have grown into a market worth trillions of dollars today.

It was the Japanese companies that adapted new technologies to commercial applications. And it laid the foundation for Japan to outpace the US in terms of GDP per capita in the 1990s. At the center of the Japan's economic rise were engineers and technicians. They include Sharp's Tadashi Sasaki, Seiko's Shinji Morozumi, and Sony's Kazuo Iwama, who have devoted their lives to semiconductors. They reinvented Japan's system semiconductor industry as creators rather than imitators.

In part II, I will take a closer look at Japan's creative inventions and how the ongoing weak yen amid the cooperation between the US and Japan could affect the dynamics of the electronics industry.

References

1. 『Inventing the Electronic Century』, by Alfred Chandler
   This masterpiece by Alfred Chandler, a professor of business history at Harvard University documents the rise and fall of big players in the American consumer electronic industry.

2. 『We Were Burning: Japanese Entrepreneurs and the Forging of the Electronic Age 1, 2』, by Bob Johnstone
   This book reads like a novel that describes the rise of the Japanese semiconductor industry. Section 3. 'Japan's Global Dominance: Imitation and Creation' of this column is actually a digest version of the book. I recommend you to read this book.

Watching out for the Resurgence of Japan's Electronics Industry (Part II)[1]

1. Japan's Global Dominance: Imitation and Creation (II)

Japan once produced over half of the world's supply of semiconductors, but now its market share fell drastically. In its prime time, Japan had the Big 6 DRAM manufacturers such as Matsushita, NEC, Fujitsu, Hitachi, Mitsubishi, and Toshiba, and also leading commercial system semiconductor makers including Sony, Sharp, Seiko, Casio, and Canon. Sanyo, a 60-year-old large-scale enterprise group in Japan, joined the semiconductor market by designing semiconductors for solar cells.

The semiconductor manufacturing, however, was not always dominated by only large-scale corporations. There have been many cases where some emerging tech companies came up with new, brilliant products to

---

[1] This column was published on February 13, 2024.

conquer the market. Let's find out the success stories of such companies.

1) Yamaha's Monopoly over the FM chips

John Chowning at Stanford University invented the frequency modulation (FM) synthesis algorithm in 1967, a method of generating sound that allows for a huge amount of control, leading to a diverse array of sounds. Interested at the news, Bell Labs' Acoustic and Behavioral Research Department invited Chowning to listen to the computer music he had created. But they did not go further than suggesting him to apply for a patent.

Instead, Stanford University's Office of Technology Licensing began the long process of courting instrument companies for Chowning. The first company contacted was the Hammond Organ, whose brand name had become synonymous with electric organs in the days. But Hammond was not fascinated by the synthesis technology. Soon after, Yamaha, a new Japanese organ maker reached out.

Yamaha, which started its business with repairing broken reed organs, released its first electronic organ in 1959.

Yasunori Mochida, the head of R&D at Yamaha, wanted a breakthrough to challenge the formidable market dominant, Hammond. For that purpose, new FM chips were needed.

Mochida sought a partnership with big tech companies that could make FM chips, but in the early days major companies like Toshiba were not into the semiconductor business. He had no choice but to develop them by himself.

In 1969, Mochida teamed up with six new college graduates and went to Junichi Nishizawa (1926-2014), an eccentric professor at Tohoku University. Nishizawa was a genius scientist who invented the PIN diode in 1949 at the age of 23, and the technology is widely used in medical imaging equipment nowadays. However, he often clashed with others, filing lawsuits against collaborating companies.

Yamaha sent the development team to Tohoku University to learn technologies, and for the young engineers Prof. Nishizawa was like Messiah. They absorbed the oddball scientist's teachings like a sponge. Meanwhile, basic manufacturing technology would be transferred under license from the US firm Philco, a subsidiary of

Ford. The young engineers succeeded in designing the IC in 18 months since the project was launched. They began producing FM chips in volume in a factory at the company's main Hamamatsu plant in 1971, around the same time when Sharp and Seiko began mass production.

Chowning was working with Yamaha to produce its first prototype based on FM synthesis. Yamaha spared no effort in developing cutting-edge technologies so as to become one the first Japanese companies to purchase stepper motors, a crucial manufacturing equipment. In 1978, the Yamaha GX-1, the first really new type of synthesizer with 50 FM chips on parallel ports was released.

In 1983, prevailing against all odds for five years after the launch of the GX-1, Yamaha finally released the DX-7, a synthesizer featuring a whole new type of FM synthesis engine. The DX-7 cost only $2,000, half the price of similar instruments in the United States. It is one of the best-selling synthesizers in history, selling more than 200,000 units. Yamaha has quickly established itself as a leading manufacturer of electronic keyboard instruments.

Among the first customers for FM chips were arcade game companies like Sega and Bally. Teenagers who were bored with entertainment machines installed in public businesses got fascinated at the new arcade games armed with the expressive and dynamic sounds with FM synthesis. After changing the future of video game sounds, the FM sound chips went on to find their way into soundboards on PS/2, Personal System/2 that is IBM's second generation of personal computers released in 1986. Millions of soundboards were sold.

By the mid-1990s, Yamaha nearly monopolized the market for FM chip technology. Yamaha has been known as a manufacturer of musical instruments and motorcycles, but it is actually one of the leading semiconductor companies in Japan. Even now that the core patents for FM synthesis has expired, Yamaha is still the global leader in the multi-billion-dollar sound card market.

2) Stanly Electric and Its Commercialization of LED

In 1962, Nick Holonyak Jr. at GE Laboratory demonstrated the world's first light-emitting diode (LED), notably creating the visible red light. However, GE failed to see that this LED would be its future replacing incandescent light bulbs. The first low-powered LEDs in the 1960s could produce only red light and were not bright enough, being only 1/100 of incandescent bulbs. Holonyak left GE in 1963 to teach at the University of Illinois and he never came back.

Monsanto researchers were deeply impressed by Holonyak's invention. Monsanto was a chemical corporation and leading producer of fertilizer, and owned phosphates mines. Phosphate is actually a raw material for gallium arsenide phosphide wafers that are used in manufacturing LEDs. Monsanto, which was looking for business opportunities in the emerging semiconductor industry, decided to take a chance to develop LEDs.

However, Monsanto was a chemical company accustomed to producing in bulk and delivering in large quantities, so their management did not like the idea of producing and selling small chips. Even worse, the LED market was highly susceptible to economic fluctuations and technological changes. In fact, LED saw its market share shrink down to 40%, replaced by LCD (liquid crystal display) in the pocket calculator market. Eventually GE and Monsanto withdrew from the LED market. Then came Stanley Electric, an unknown Japanese company on stage.

Stanley Electric was a manufacturer of automobile light

bulbs. The company was worried about what would happen to them if a better way to produce light came along. They would go out of business as they were producing only tungsten light bulbs for automobile lamps. Toru Teshima, an engineer of Stanley Electric went to seek help outside in 1969. The expert they turned to, was again Dr. Nishizawa of Tohuku University.

Toshiba was the front runner in Japan, in the competition for LED technology. Toshiba engineers had learned the processing of gallium phosphide (GaP) from Bell Labs. And other big companies like Matsushita, NEC, Sanyo, and Sharp were also making LEDs based on Monsanto's product. Teshima was getting anxious.

But in 1973 Teshima's faith in Nishizawa finally paid off. When the first batch of elements produced in a newly-installed furnace was applied with an electric current, they glowed red. Over the next three years, Stanley Electric kept refining its technology and successfully produced the world's brightest red LED. However, when it came to selling the product, the market's response was lukewarm. There were plenty of leading suppliers like Toshiba or Matsushita, why buy from an untested latecomer. But at the 1976 Los Angeles Trade Fairs, Stanley Electric exhibited its

LED products, side by side with the products from major companies. They outshined its competitors - giving a complete victory for Stanley Electric at last.

Stanley Electric came up with an idea of LED graphic equalizers for the sound system. They moved like dancing to the music sound. People were captivated by the new equalizer, of which graphs seemed to be pulsating as dynamically as a live animal. The 1970s Nissan sports car "Fairlady", which took the world by storm had the LED brake lights made by Stanley Electric.

However, to replace light bulbs completely, LEDs had to produce a white light. Red light alone was not enough. Creating white light required a combination of three colors - red, green, and blue light. Green and other colors joined the LED revolution soon, but blue remained an elusive holy grail despite the strenuous efforts by numerous scientists. By the time when leading companies like RCA, Matsushita, and Hewlett-Packard were about to throw in the towel, a young engineer in an unexpected corner of the world tried his wits and succeeded in creating the first-luminosity blue LED. It took a quarter of a century since Nick Holonyak's invention of red-light diodes.

3) Nobel Prize-Awarded Blue LED

In fact, it was RCA's Jacques Pankov who created the first blue LED. He created LEDs of various colors, including blue, using gallium nitride semiconductors in 1971. But after conducting a series of market study, the company's marketing team advised against LED with a variety of colors, suggesting to focus more on lowering the price of LEDs. RCA slashed the budget of the research and the blue LED project was officially dead.

Nichia Chemical began its business as a small fluorescent materials manufacturer, located in Annan, Shikoku, the smallest of the four main islands of Japan. It developed a new type of calcium phosphate, a raw material of phosphors for fluorescent lamps and supplied them to large corporations. Nichia had pursued research and development of its own, unlike large corporations that relied on technology licensing from foreign firms, and the light emitted from its fluorescent materials were 20% brighter than the lights from those made by its titanic competitors.

Nichia kept expanding its business and got to produce tri-color - red, blue and green - phosphors in 1971, for coating the inside of a cathode ray tube of color televisions. This move was a huge success, allowing Nichia to capture 50% of the Japanese domestic market and 25% of the global market.

Shuji Nakamura studied electrical engineering at a local university, then decided to stay in his hometown and joined Nichia, a small chemical company near his hometown in April 1979. He was under the wing of Nichia's founder and president, Nobuo Ogawa, who more or less gave him free rein for his research. Nakamura started his research laboratory for himself and began his quest to develop a bright blue LED.

Ogawa gave Nakamura his unwavering support. He bought the young researcher equipment, financed him to study at the University of Florida, invested several million dollars in his research projects, and arranged an industry-academic collaborative program for him. After performing countless experiments, Nakamura finally made a breakthrough with the use of a gallium nitride semiconductor to create blue LEDs in September 1992. In early 1993, Nakamura grew a thin film of gallium nitride crystal and produced a blue LED that was 100 times brighter than any blue LED ever produced to that point and as bright as Stanley Electric's red LED. This was a wonderful scientific discovery made possible after 15 years since he joined Nichia. His inventions have not only sent a shock wave through the global industry but also turned physicists around the world upside down. They wondered "which university is Dr. Shuji Nakamura from?"

Blue LED has revolutionized data storage as well. Developing blue laser ahead of rivals could enable a company to jumpstart in the highly promising optical data storage technology. The amount of data that can be stored in an optical disc is related to the wavelength of the laser employed. The shorter the wavelength of the light, the closer the data tracks can be placed on the disk, giving more room for more data. This enabled manufacturers to make storage devices by far smaller. An audio CD under a red laser could only hold up to 74 minutes of Beethoven's symphony No.9, also known as the 'Choral'. However, a blue laser could accommodate recordings of the complete Beethoven symphonies from No. 1 to No. 9.

In 2014, Shuji Nakamura became the first Nobel Prize winner in Physics for his pioneering and groundbreaking achievement made when he was a young engineer with bachelor's degree. Now he is a professor in a US university.

4) Japan Dominating the World of Consumer Electronics[2]

When Thomson, the French state-owned electronics company acquired the RCA Corporation In 1988, the death knell was rung for the American consumer electronics industry. Thomson was nationalized in 1982 as part of the social and economic program during President Mitterrand's Socialist government. And it grew fast by carrying out large-scale mergers and acquisitions of European electronics companies. But it became inoperative suffering heavy losses of billions of francs year after year in the 1990s.

Philips, the only European consumer electronics company that had survived the World War II, went down the same path. Its innovation center in Eindhoven, Netherlands was once as comparable as to those of RCA and Sony, and introduced the CD player jointly developed with Sony,

---

[2] The term consumer electronics or home electronics must have originated from the equipment for everyday use, typically in private homes like TVs, radios, and telephones. Now that they are used in wider range of environments including offices and mobile environments, the term is no longer relevant. Rather 'commercial electronics' sounds more pertinent, then it would come to encompass the computer industry. So better not to use it yet. Therefore, this column employs the term 'consumer electronics industry', as widely referred to in the academia.

reaping a huge success. However, Philips failed to come up with next innovative products and ended up recording an unprecedented loss of $2.7 billion in 1990. The Dutch electronics giant moved its headquarters to Amsterdam and has transformed its portfolio to become a lighting and health technology company. The consumer electronics industry in Europe came to an end[3], leaving its remains in Eindhoven.

Japan has come to dominate the world market in the mid-1990s. Only Japanese companies had the ability to reinvest its huge profits from previous product sales into developing new products. Only they have built the entire value chain of essential materials, parts, equipment, and services. And only they were able to run a vast research network near Tokyo and Osaka.

---

3) The demise of the European electronics industry is a topic that requires a more in-depth look. It will be dealt with later in a separate column.

2. The Decline of the Japanese Consumer Electronics

The decline of the Japanese consumer electronics began with the release of the Apple's iPhone in 2007. Before the introduction of the iPhone, mobile phones focused on calling and texting and users could take rudimentary snap shots. The iPhone, however, completely reshaped the market. It was a revolutionary new mobile phone taking advantage of computing technologies that the US had accumulated over 60 years of the postwar period. The iPhone wasn't just a mobile phone, it was the first mobile computer.

The iPhone also incorporated all of the consumer electronics technologies that Japan had developed in the same postwar era such as Sony image sensor, Seiko's low-power C-MOS technology, Sharp TFT-LCD and touch screen technology, Stanley Electric and Nichia Chemical's LED, Yamaha FM chip, and Panasonic batteries.

The problem was that the iPhone ate up almost all of the markets that Japan had been dominating. It wiped out the markets of video camcorder and digital still camera. It devastated the Japanese watch manufacturers, allowing

Swiss luxury watchmakers to make a comeback. As music and VOD (Video on Demand; YouTube) services became available on the iPhone, the demand for an audio system, CD and DVD players as well as storage devices quickly disappeared.

A bigger challenge came from the micronization process of semiconductors. When it comes to a desktop computer, there was no big difference between IBM PCs and IBM compatible clones made by smaller competitors. And people were not willing to open their wallets for a thinner, lighter, better-looking desktop IBM PC. As long as they function similarly, cheaper clones were more popular. Iconic American PC manufacturers went out of business one after another.

However, when cell phones became hand-held computers, demands for thinner, lighter, and longer-lasting smartphones skyrocketed. A smartphone has almost become an accessory like jewelry in the way of expressing oneself. When new smartphones are released in 1-2 years, people rush to get one, drawn to the latest features and improvements. Smartphones are getting thinner and lighter while offering high image quality. To make a compact and durable smartphone, you need nanometer-scale circuits, making them as thin as possible to 30, 20, and down to 10 nanometers.

A clear path to success for corporations was to focus on miniaturization process and reducing power consumption, rather than developing a new system IC. To most companies, investing in the development of a new system IC was like an account receivable to get paid in the distant future, but the miniaturization process meant an immediate cash payment. While the Japanese excelled in investing in the future, the Korean and Taiwanese were good at reaping immediate profits. The Japanese companies were also keen on quick return, but the US sanctions against Japanese semiconductors since 1985 have kept Japan from joining in the microtechnology competition.

Korea survived the fierce competition for miniaturization of semiconductor memory. Taiwan rose from a contract chipmaker whose survival was in doubt to the front runner in foundry, receiving orders from Apple and fabless companies around the world. Korean and Taiwanese companies have grown into large gigantic corporations by making the most of miniaturization.

The Japanese consumer electronics industry collapsed

entirely. Aiwa was acquired by a US company in 2006, and Sanyo was sold to China's Haier in 2012. Toshiba's white goods business was sold off to Midea in 2016 and its TV business to Hisense in 2017. Sharp was taken over by Taiwan's Foxconn in 2016. Only Sony and Matsushita are left in the consumer electrics market, but remain primarily for domestic supply.

3. Transformation of Japanese Electronics Industry

Despite the collapse of major consumer electronics companies, Japanese system IC companies are still thriving, as can be seen in Sony, Seiko, Yamaha, and Canon. As the IC supply chain is littered with nearly irreplaceable players, they set prices and supply conditions.

A majority of the fallen large consumer electronics manufacturers like Matsushita, Hitachi, Toshiba, and Mitsubishi are now active in the production of industrial electric equipment and components. Japan is one of the first countries in the world to face an aging and decreasing population. Amid the strong yen and in the wake of globalization, Japanese factories have spent the past 30 years streamlining operations and reducing energy consumption in order to compete with Chinese factories. Thereby it has brought about great advancement in industrial automation and robotics.

In late January, I visited the 34th Tokyo Electronics Expo (NEPCON). The exhibition hall was filled with automation equipment and robots from about 1,000 Japanese electronics companies. Although there is no cosmopolitan glamor as in CES in Las Vegas, NEPCON was invigorated with a sense of practical tension among Japanese engineers. If CES is something like a masquerade show in a grand ballroom, NEPCON is a low-key show focusing more on serious technological talk in a backroom.

Japan has become a global powerhouse of robots and factory automation systems, providing full turnkey solutions to reduce robot-related costs and establish automated assembly lines. What does this mean? In the era of globalization over the past 30 years, large companies in the West have headed to China in search of cheap labor. Japan, the factory of the old world, had to reduce labor and energy costs to compete with China, the factory of the new world. In truth, Japanese robots had been competing with cheap Chinese labor.

Amid the US-China hegemony rivalry and geopolitical crisis, foreign companies have for years been shifting production away from China to the United States. But in the US workers are scarce and expensive, and do not stay for long. Gig economy jobs like Uber driver, delivery rider, etc. are out there alluring them with flexibility and autonomy. Even unskilled servers in restaurants receive 20% of the total bill as a tip.

In the near future American factories will be run by Japanese automation systems and robots. Factories all around the world will have no choice but to buy Japanese robots to compete. Korean factories are no exception. The United States and Germany attempted to tackle the challenges coming from aging and shrinking population by increasing immigration, while Japan tried to solve the problem with automation. Japan is the only country in the world that is industrially ready to deal with the demographic decline.

4. Japan, Poised to Overtake China

Now, let's take a closer look at electronics industry on the global map. Big tech companies in the US are only claiming its share in the computing business like the generative AI, and Europe's electronics industry has disappeared without trace. After 30 years of arduous efforts, the Japanese electronics sector has gone through drastic structural transformation from consumer electronics to industrial electronics, with only a few system IC companies remaining. Korea has only two or three globally competitive chip companies, but they have already grown too big in size to adapt to the rapidly changing market needs with agility. The miniaturization race that was going on for the past 20 years has cut the size of chips continually down to 5-, 3- and 2-nanometers, and now has its finish line almost in sight.

No new system ICs have been developed ever since the release of the Apple's iPhone. This is because the technology R&D clusters in Tokyo and Osaka have come to a standstill. On top of that, semiconductor technologies have been driven solely towards miniaturization and low power consumption. Now, there is only one place in the world that has the resources and manpower to develop next-generation system ICs - China. It has been siphoning electronics technologies of the United States, Japan, Korea and Taiwan over the past 30 years.

The biggest concern right now is, which will be the first to commercialize 3-nano and 2-nano technologies among the top industrial players and which will dominate the market for EUV lithography equipment. Some critics say that China's semiconductor industry is doomed due to the US sanctions against China and also that Huawei's new 5G phones are riddled with problems. But others say that it is almost impossible, as Tim Cook admitted, for Apple to leave China and that Shenzhen in Guangdong Province has earned global recognition as a dynamic innovation hub, dazzling visitors. How do you think future will unfold?

In fact, China's grip on electronics manufacturing will be hard to break. Although it used to be a subcontractor for Korea, the United States, Japan, and Taiwan, it has learned from its efforts and developed by leaps and bounds over the last 30 years. In the electronics industry M&A is not necessarily a key solution for growth. It was proven in the past examples that the UK, France, Germany and Italy had made efforts to develop its electronics industry on the national level, but to no avail. As the history of the Japanese electronics industry shows, the development of the electronics industry takes geeks, geniuses, greedy entrepreneurs, and stubborn engineers, who are ready to take on challenges and never give up.

China's industrial policy for emerging industries is likely to walk two paths at the same time. First, strong regulations as demonstrated recently in the Chinese government's crackdown on its Big Tech, Fintech and education platform companies. Second, it will remain supportive of creative entrepreneurs, encouraging development of new and innovative products. Creative inventions do not necessarily require state-of-the-art EUV lithography machines. Successful businessmen, engineers, and inventors will become rich and be treated as national heroes. ("To get rich is glorious. Let's some people get rich first.", the catchy slogan of Deng Xiaoping, the chief architect of China's reform and opening-up). China's aspiration for global domination, after all, hinges on the innovative entrepreneurship.

Let's say

《 A Chinese company releases an innovative new product called 'X Glasses' after a hefty investment and persistent R&D efforts. It looks just like regular glasses, but BTS music comes out of its earphones and holograms of BTS members pop out and dance right in front of you. And it also allows you to have virtual conversations with BTS members using AI technology. The BTS ARMYs around the world go crazy about it, and more than 100 million units are sold a year.

This puts the US government in trouble. It can get public consent on banning the import of BYD's electric vehicles on the grounds that they pose a threat to the national security and industrial base. But it cannot regulate the import of the glasses. X-Glasses, small and light, can be indirectly imported and easily smuggled. Or you can even buy one on your business trips overseas. China's GDP is expected to increase by 0.5% this year due to the huge success of X-Glasses. 》

To counterbalance the vast industrial clusters in Shenzhen and Shanghai, Washington has turned its eyes to Japan. There are 12,000 Japanese companies operating in China, and thousands of them are electronics companies. They must return to Japan. To make it happen, it is required to improve their profit margins and make them cash-rich so that they can make investments. New life must be breathed into the lackluster R&D clusters in Tokyo and Osaka. An alliance between the revitalized Japanese electronics companies and American IT companies, would empower the US and Japan to regain the dominance in the global electronics market. Japan's resurgence is in the US's national interest. To that end, the weak yen is the first step.

5. Path Ahead of Us

As was mentioned in the introduction, economic growth is defined as an increase in added value produced in primary, secondary, and tertiary industries. Added value of a product increases when you sell it for more than it costs you to produce. Simply put, you need to develop a new, innovative product. Some critics say, citing the multiplier effect theory, that growth occurs only when consumption increases or that government subsidies, either received or consumed, contributes to economic growth in general. But it is a blatant lie or at least an exaggeration.

The essence of corporate investment is not the investment in factory facilities, but the fundings in R&D that involves a risk-taking. When R&D efforts give rise to new, groundbreaking technologies or products that captivate consumers around the world, companies will invest more in facilities and hire more workers on their own initiative. In other words, R&D should come before the investment in factory facilities.

Expanding fiscal spending and easing monetary policy does not lead to economic growth. Japan's Lost 30 Years is a clear evidence. The history of the Japanese electronics industry attests that economic growth is something achievable only through intense and long R&D competition among unyielding entrepreneurs.

No one knows what type of research and development competition would take place among the three countries, the United States, Japan, and China in the global electronics industry in the future. In the midst of the fierce competition among the three countries for the world dominance, what strategy should Korean companies employ? Let us think it over by looking at two cases below.

The original technology for EUV, an advanced photolithography technique using extreme ultraviolet was developed in the United States. When the US was considering licensing the technology overseas, the number one candidate was, of course, Nikon in Japan. This was because Nikon had a 90% market share of cutting-edge DUV equipment. However, the US Department of Defense was against the idea because rising Japan was considered a threat to the national security. In the end, the technology was transferred to the Dutch company ASML.

Recording billions of dollars of losses during the subprime mortgage crisis, GM was set to sell 50% of its stake in its spun-off company Aptiv, an autonomous vehicle supplier, to a Chinese company. But the US Department of Defense came in the way, citing national security concerns that Aptive's technologies could be used for unmanned tanks and unmanned armored vehicles. GM sold its stock to Hyundai Motors instead.

The United States and Japan are still leading technological evolutions around the world. Of course, you never know if a creative engineer on the remote southeastern coast of China may shock the world with some revolutionary inventions. It is up to our government and corporations to make choices who to join hands with and which way to go.

COMPUTEX TAIPEI 2024 From a Geopolitical Perspective[1]

1. Prospering Taiwan

Taiwan is an island caught in the middle of U.S.-China power struggle, where the core interests of the two countries clash and nightmare scenarios are rife over its future. The geopolitical anxiety across the Strait is in fact greater than that between South and North Korea: From China's blockade of Taiwan, a cross-strait military confrontation, to interfering the Taiwanese election for regime change and China's United Front campaign against Taiwan. As the self-ruled island is dwarfed by the gigantic mainland in all aspects - population, economy, military strength, and diplomacy, the sense of crisis is by no means exaggerated.

Despite geopolitical uncertainty and instability, however, Taiwan is prospering. Over the 10 years from 2013 to 2023, Taiwan grew by 3.2% annually while Korea recorded an

---

[1] This column was published on July 5, 2024.

average annual growth rate of 2.6%. As a result, tide has turned between the two countries in terms of GDP per capita for the first time in 18 years (Korea $32,237, Taiwan $32,811).

What is noteworthy is that Taiwan's economic success is something that can hardly be explained by common sense macroeconomics. First, once capital and labor input-driven growth is over, a country's economic growth rate should gradually decrease. However, Taiwan's growth rate has actually increased and is expected to be 3.4% in 2024, reaching the highest level among advanced economies with incomes of more than $30,000.

Second, as an economy expands its manufacturing sector with low added value shrinks and high-end service industries take up a larger proportion. But Taiwan's manufacturing sector grew from 29.1% in 2013 to 34.2% in 2023, by more than 5%. The value-added rate of manufacturing in Taiwan was reported at 32.5%, which was about 4% higher than Korea's 28.7% (as of 2022). It is indicative of the fact that advanced economies can keep recording dynamic growth as long as they have internationally competitive high-tech manufacturing and continue to make technological innovations.

Taiwan's manufacturing industry was once comprised of mostly small and medium-sized enterprises that were mostly subcontractors to the United States and Japan. But over the course of the last 10 years they have transformed into large corporations with international competitiveness. A number of new innovative companies emerged, such as TSMC and UMC in foundries, MediaTek, Novatech, and Realtek in fabless IC designing, ASE in semiconductor assembly, Foxconn which is a global OEM, Quanta Computer, ASUS, and ACER in computer manufacturing, and Delta Electronics producing electronic components. TSMC's market capitalization is almost twice that of Samsung Electronics, exceeding KRW 1,000 trillion. And the combined market capitalization of Taiwan's Big 3 fabless chipmakers, MediaTek, Novatech, and Realtek exceeds that of Hyundai Motors and Kia Motors. More importantly, the Korean government has rolled up its sleeves to resolve the nagging issue of 'Korea discount', but Taiwanese companies which seem to be by far riskier than Korean counterparts, don't have the same problem.

2. Taiwan, the Center of AI Revolution

AI revolution is unfolding in two directions. One is to develop a Large Language Model (LLM), in which all the American cloud service providers (MS, Google, Amazon) are competing. Cloud service providers are investing tens of billions of dollars, hopeful of gaining industrial hegemony just as Google overwhelmingly dominates the search engine market.

This is not a business of Taiwanese firms. But most of AI semiconductors are supplied by NVIDIA, the pioneer of GPU-accelerated computing led by Jansen Huang who is an American born in Taiwan. On top of that, NVIDIA's AI chips for data centers are made by Taiwanese Semiconductor Manufacturing Company (TSMC).

The other is developing AI-enabled smart devices like PCs, mobile phones, and servers. In order for AI functions to be performed on the device itself without an internet connection, high-performance, high-capacity, low-power AI semiconductors are required. This triggered a 'war without gunfire' in the PC market. The global PC market has been on the decline, losing momentum to mobile phones. Since Apple's release of iPhone in 2007, mobile phones have become hand-held personal computers, and industry players have been waging a fierce battle for better design, resolution, data speed, camera sensors and battery performance, and for lighter and thinner phones. As a result, their innovative efforts increased value-added and paid off as consumers opened their wallets. In the meantime, the desktop and laptop computer markets have been struggling with an increasing number of consumers turning their backs.

Until now, PCs have been office supplies and entertainment devices that allow users to use the Internet and enjoy games and videos, but personal AI is about to change completely how you use computers. On May 20, 2024, Microsoft unveiled a new generation of PCs under the name Copilot+ PC, heralding a new AI PC era. Copilot+ PC developed in collaboration with PC manufacturers is set to incorporate the latest Open AI GPT model, ChatGPT 4o.

An AI-powered PC performs functions that were impossible on traditional PCs. It can create videos, pictures, and music requested by users, and also generate documents and even translate them. Apple and Google are poised to provide AI app platforms, as they opened a hugely lucrative business of app stores through their mobile app platforms. Engineers and designers at startups will be empowered to leverage AI-driven tools for boosting their creativity and generating profits. Simply put, a new AI ecosystem is built.

Over the past several decades, Intel and AMD have been dominating the central processing units (CPU) marekt. PC companies around the world bought chips from Intel and AMD and produced PCs in manufacturing sites in Taiwan and China. At Computex 2024 in Taiwan, Qualcomm has made it clear that it is actively entering the AI PC market by unveiling a new AI chip, Snapdragon X Elite. Qualcomm's new chips will be incorporated into Copilot+ PCs together with Intel's Lunar Lake chips. AMD as well is expected to release its new AI chip, Strix Point 2. NVIDIA, the world's biggest fabless company, may soon join in the next-generation AI chip market.

Intel, the king of the semiconductor industry has taken a significant step to outsource the production of some of its chips to TSMC, breaking its 40-year-long rule of keeping the manufacturing of its best semiconductors in-house. Fearing that outsourcing could result in leaving the door open for competitors, Intel dedicated its factories exclusively to its own chips since 1985 when it released its revolutionary 80386 CPU. In order to uphold its production capacity to meet the growing demand, Intel had to withdraw from the market for dynamic random access memory, DRAM which it had pioneered. Such Intel has committed to TSMC, a Taiwanese foundry, the production of three new AI chips - Lunar Lake, Xeon 6 Processor, and Gaudi3 AI Accelerator.

AI-capable PCs are forecast to account for 80% of global PC shipments by 2028. While both Intel and AMD use the X86 architecture, Qualcomm, a new challenger in the industry, offers the power-efficient and very compelling ARM-based solutions. It is yet to see which one will win over consumers, the high-end processing speed of X86 or the low power consumption of ARM. To keep AMD and Qualcomm at bay, Intel is in desperate need of the 3-nanometer process. This explains the Intel's decision to outsource some of its chip manufacturing to TSMC.

The new AI chips of Intel, AMD, and Qualcomm's will be delivered to major manufacturers, such as ASUS, Acer in Taiwan; Lenovo in China; Dell, HP in USA; and Samsung. Most PCs of these companies are made in China. Collaboration with PC companies is vital for semiconductor companies to get ahead in the AI PC race, as demand for AI chips is going sky-high. The same goes for the server industry. Intel's Gaudi3 is supplied to 10 AI server manufacturing partners including ASUS, Foxconn, Gigabyte, Inventec, Quanta, Wistron, Supermicro in Taiwan; Dell, HPE in USA; and Lenovo in China - of which 7 are Taiwanese companies.

With Taiwan standing big on the tech industry map, the CEOs of the world's chip heavyweights, Intel, AMD, Qualcomm and NVIDIA, flocked to Computex Taipei 2024 in early June. The U.S. government passed the Inflation Reduction Act (IRA) to bring semiconductor manufacturing back to the U.S., but NVIDIA and AMD are planning to build their new R&D centers in Taiwan. NVIDIA CEO Jensen Huang, underscoring the importance of his home country, declared in the keynote speech at Computex 2024. "Taiwan is the center of AI revolution."

3. U.S. Semiconductor Industry Entrapped in Taiwan

Both semiconductor and computer industries were born in the USA. Fairchild Semiconductor and IBM were pioneers of each industry, from which numerous start-ups spun off. Located in the outskirts of San Francisco, these tech companies manufactured their innovative products in their fabs, financing from R&D funds of the Department of Defense, investments from friends and family, and bank loans.

However, in the era of higher interest rates under Federal Reserve Chairman Paul Volcker in the 1980s, these tech startups have turned to new financing methods. When interest rates are high, investors get impatient and they tend to invest less and be anxious to pull their money out of markets quickly. Here came venture capital. It is a type of financing startup companies helping investors exit after some time, typically three to four years after their initial investment, by initiating an initial public offering (IPO).

Start-ups in Silicon Valley struggled to survive a funding crunch. For the cash-strapped new enterprises, R&D outweighs production, and so they have no choice but to go fabless. Start-ups found an easy way out with Morris Chang, former senior executive at Texas Instruments and who happens to be CEO of Taiwan Semiconductor Manufacturing Company (TSMC) which he founded in 1987 with government funding. It marked the beginning of separation of design and fabrication, which became known as the foundry model, with fabless chipmakers outsourcing to semiconductor foundries.

American companies are the brain, Taiwanese companies are the brawn to execute the orders from the brain. Chips are intermediate goods used in the production of electronic devices such as smartphones and laptops. Similarly, fabricating process was divided further, such that Taiwan orchestrates the fabrication process and final goods are made in Chinese factories. Thus came an international supply chain between the United States, Taiwan, and China.

It seemed to hold true, until recently, that the United States' dominance in the semiconductor market is rock-solid with the source technology in hand and top fabless semiconductor companies are still American companies. Intel is one of the leading companies that both design and manufacture leading -edge logic chips, and fabless chip giants such as AMD, Qualcomm, NVIDIA and Broadcom are American-based. No problem at all.

Main contractors of any project need to work with multiple subcontractors. Samsung Electronics, LG Electronics, Hyundai Motors, and Kia Motors, for instance, operate their businesses by hiring subcontractors. A main contractor must not only provide design drawings, but also be able to offer technical guidance and transfer of knowhows. However, most of fabless companies had never made the chip and just outsourced production to Taiwanese companies, without any idea about the foundry process. They thought they could get the chip supplied at reduced costs from a number of foundries in Taiwan and Singapore competing one another.

The foundry industry was no exception to the harsh condition that productivity and production yield single-handedly determine overall costs in the highly competitive semiconductor market. TSMC's most notable achievements of cutting-edge 12-inch wafers and miniaturization of transistors helped it solidify its dominance. It has pushed up its global market share in legacy products to 60% and is producing about 90% of the world's high-tech semiconductors with expertise in ultra-fine chip fabrication by using incredibly expensive EUV lithography tools. The main contractors thought they would be benefitting from the competition among subcontractors, but ended up being subject to a monopoly. American fabless companies that have been preoccupied with cost-cutting and efficiency, are eventually entrapped by TSMC, which has become a linchpin of the global economy with its remarkable productivity.

Besides foundry, Taiwan has also made substantial progress in going fabless. Taiwan's MediaTek, reporting considerable $13.2 billion in sales for 2023, is the world's 5th largest fabless semiconductor company, and Realtek with sales of $3 billion and Novatech are catching up fast. They are large suppliers of smartphone parts to Chinese companies.

How have these fabless companies emerged as a powerhouse in the fabless industry? A company obtains a new technology by; ① officially licensing the source technology, ② recruiting elite engineers from leading companies, or ③ using 'any other means available.' What it means is left to your imagination.

As the world's largest semiconductor foundry specialist, TSMC says, "We do not compete with customers within the foundry." In other words, the business partners' trade secrets are absolutely safe with them. And this explains bleak outlook for Samsung Electronics' foundry business with Intel. Customers are reluctant to entrust foundry process to IDMs, Integrated Device Manufacturers that both design and manufacture chips, for fear of technology theft.

The knowledge that TSMC has accumulated while working with world-class fabless companies is what Taiwanese companies are avidly after. No matter how strict TSMC's information security defense is, Taiwanese and Chinese engineers who share a common inheritance of blood and language, are inevitably connected with each other by either blood or academic ties, or fellowship at work. It is not uncommon for engineers to move from one project to another. In fact, job transfers and cooperation within industrial clusters are persistent. Informal brainstorming sessions take place in restaurants, bars, baseball stadiums, and golf courses. The same goes for New Jersey and Silicon Valley in the United States, Tokyo and Osaka in Japan, and Suwon and Gumi Industrial Complex in Korea.

Even worse, many of the executives at American fabless companies are Chinese. Chip giant NVIDIA's Jensen Huang and AMD CEO Lisa Su are of Taiwanese descent, and Broadcom CEO Hock Tan is a Chinese-American born in Malaysia. Qualcomm would not be able to advance into AI PC market without a partnership of TSMC and Taiwanese computer companies. Apple has been urging Foxconn, a

Taiwanese multinational electronics contract manufacturer to move out of China for several years, but Foxconn has neither the intention nor the ability to do so. Although Foxconn has the largest share in iPhone assembly among Apple suppliers, building a huge electronic component ecosystem in India or Mexico is simply out of range. It is unlikely that Apple/ Foxconn will replicate what Samsung has achieved in Vietnam.

A major growth engine for Taiwan's fabless companies have been strong demand from Chinese mobile phone manufacturers, and China's semiconductor and electronics industries are trying to emulate Taiwan's tech prowess. If Hong Kong has been the most important source of international capital for the Mainland, Taiwan is like the crown jewel for China's electronics industry. No matter what regulatory measures are implemented by the U.S., such as the CHIPS & Science Act to keep chip funds out of China, time and momentum is on China's side as Taiwan and China are industrially inseparable. China wants to keep Taiwan as is and does not want the jewel in its crown to be tarnished.

4. How to Deal with Taiwan?

British daily Financial Times[2] reports that Chinese president Xi Jinping in a meeting with Ursla von der Leyen, head of European Commission in April 2023 said that Washington was trying to "goad Beijing into attacking Taiwan, but he would not take the bait". If 'Made in China 2025", an initiative to upgrade Chinese industry is to be successful, Beijing has no reason to invade Taiwan from an industrial perspective.

Industry is a fundamental driver for the economic growth of a nation. Japan evolved into a global economic powerhouse with its automobile and electronics industries in the mid-1990s. Likewise, if China proves successful in its efforts to develop electric vehicle and semiconductor industries, it might overtake the United States as the world's largest economy.

As witnessed in Beijing Motor Show 2024, Chinese electric vehicles and batteries have notable advantages in terms of raw materials, technology, and marketability. The next step is to enter export markets, and its promising candidate is Europe. But the European Commission has

---

2) See June 17, 2024 Financial Times, page 4

raised tariffs up to almost 48% on electronic cars shipped from China to counteract what it called unfair subsidies received by Chinese EV makers. Immediately afterward, Germany's Economy Minister Robert Habeck rushed to Beijing and explained that these are not punitive tariffs and are not something Germany hoped for.

In the end, however, EU tariffs won't halt Chinese EVs' advance. Germany must sell Volkswagen cars, and France wine and cosmetics in the Chinese market. Italy also needs to sell fabric for furniture and suits and attract Chinese tourists. European countries are vulnerable in the face of the spending power of China's emerging middle class, which is estimated at roughly 250 million people. Chinese electric vehicles and batteries will take over a significant share of the European market.

What remains now in China's bid to lead the world is the semiconductor and electronics industry. The United States is patching up controls over exports of high-performance semiconductors and equipment to China with the enactment of the CHIPS & Science Act, but U.S. reliance on Taiwan chips is growing bigger as it lacks foundry capability. TSMC announced that it will build a semiconductor facility in the U.S. soil, but the U.S.

production capacity of advanced chips will not be more than 4% until 2027. Currently, Taiwan produces 91% of the world's most advanced processor chips, and that is expected to remain at 85% until 2027. The more advanced the process, the higher the proportion of Taiwanese production.

Taiwanese companies are tightly interwoven with Chinese mobile phone and electronic companies. The United States can keep Taiwanese companies under control with regulatory measures, but it has little or no control over the rights and freedom of Taiwanese people. Even Intel, after almost 60 years of a near-monopoly in the server chip market, outsourced chip production to TSMC under increasing pressure from the emerging AI PC. Americans must have seen it clearly at COMPUTEX 2024: It is out of the question to separate Taiwan's semiconductor industry from China's industry.

An empire does not reach out foreign countries for advanced technology. What it cannot have must be destroyed. It is the imperialistic United States, not China that wants to destroy Taiwan's industry. That's what Xi Jinping is saying in his remark about U.S. trying to 'goad' Beijing into war.

5. On 'U.S. for Security, China for Economy'

Are the U.S. and China on a collision course over Taiwan? Security experts argue that Taiwan has its stake in the peace and stability of Korean Peninsula, and vice versa. What options are available for South Korea? There must be discussions going on in the diplomatic and security circles. It is not the point of discussion in this column. It focuses on how to set up Korea-China relationship from an economic perspective.

Some say that even if the U.S. and China competition for global hegemony intensifies further, Washington has no choice but to remain dependent on Chinese manufacturing. And it means that a certain level of cooperation between Korea and China is unavoidable, signaling that Korea should move in the direction of bolstering economic ties with China. This is version 2.0 of the past Korean government's strategy of 'U.S. for security, China for economy.'

However, economic cooperation with China requires a careful juggling in the midst of China's attempt to rise to great power. Once a Korean politician, an ardent advocate of economic cooperation with China, claimed that "It's like holding onto the back of a horse to travel a thousand miles." The past 30 years of strong economic growth of Korea has been largely benefited from the rapid development in China. But now globalization is coming to an end, and U.S.-China relations are in a linear downward spiral. China's economic dominance no longer means an opportunity for prosperity for Korea. An empire pursues prosperity for its own, not for the peripheral states.

The Joseon Dynasty suffered from constant pressure from the Ming and Qing empires for over 500 years. Even now few neighboring countries of modern China are left in prosperity. This is neither due to Chinese traditional hegemonic view of the world, nor the peculiarities of communism. The modern free world was not different, either. When the British Empire was in her prime, the Irish, whilst being part of the empire starved to death due to the potato famine and emigrated to the United States, resulting in the dramatic decrease in population. The United States is also on the lookout for rise of prosperous powers in North and South America. Invariably, every empire has prosperous center and declining peripheries. For that is the key to a long-lasting empire.

As was experienced in the THAAD crisis, economic

decoupling with China can make it hard for Korean enterprises today. However, over the course of time, Korea's next generations will live in a country, economically prosperous, independent and with self-respect as part of rich Western civilization. On the site of COMPUTEX in Taiwan, observing Taiwan's semiconductor industry thrive hand in hand with China keeping the U.S. on leash, I could not help but to ponder this elusive paradox.

References

1. 『Hyundai Motor Securities' Review on the Visit to COMPUTEX 2024 and Corporations in Taiwan』, published on June 14, 2024.
   The author visited COMPUTEX Taipei 2024, courtesy of Hyundai Motor Securities Center Director Noh Geun-chang. Section 2. 'Taiwan, the Center of AI Revolution' of this column, in particular, is greatly indebted to the review. I would like to take this opportunity to express my gratitude.